POPULAR GAMES AND THE UNIVERSAL IDENTITY

An Egyptian Prospect

IMAN MAHRAN

POPULAR GAMES AND THE UNIVERSAL IDENTITY

An Egyptian Prospect

GALDA VERLAG 2018

Bibliografische Information der Deutschen Nationalbibliothek
Die Deutsche Nationalbibliothek verzeichnet diese Publikation in der Deutschen Nationalbibliografie; detaillierte bibliografische Daten sind im Internet über http://dnb.ddb.de abrufbar.

© 2018 Galda Verlag, Glienicke
English translation by Dr. Eman Mahmoud Elesawy; Lecturer at Faculty of Alsun Minia University
Direct all inquiries to Galda Verlag, Franz-Schubert-Str. 61, 16548 Glienicke, Germany

ISBN 978-3-96203-047-6 (Print)
ISBN 978-3-96203-048-3 (Ebook)

To my play partner....who shares everything with me
The Joseph of his age,
The soft breeze of my life,
My son ..my wild flower

CONTENTS

2 THE PSYCHOLOGICAL AND EDUCATIONAL ASPECTS OF POPULAR GAMES

4 GAMES AND THE UNIVERSAL IDENTITY

5 GAMES AND DIGITAL TECHNOLOGY

INTRODUCIO

Each community has its own integral and unchangeable features which represent a vital part of it. They are a part of the collective sedimentary layers of the society. Numerous details of traditions, daily life norms and forms that organize the society are also incorporated.

Games are remnants of the ancient methods that existed in several domains of everyday life which passed very long phases of erosion that only the remnants are implicitly practiced by the young.

Women have a large role in these aspects. They are the holders of this folkloric heritage and the child's partner in his childhood and play.

Popular games are the product of the society's culture. They are concrete movements in place and time. There are games that can be played and spread widely and easily because their tools are available.

Ancient Egypt, India and China are among the most ancient places where popular games were practiced.

Popular games reflect the cultural history of the community. In some cases, they are the remains of the civilization of the land upon which the player stands. Games provide a positive outlet of energy. They are a vital human function in a performative form.

Playing has been historically associated with the expansion and transfer of human knowledge. With the increasing population on earth, knowledge accumulated. A part of it was epitomized while the other disappeared. Consequently, popular games became the common and shared folkloric factor passed over from ancient civilizations.

Games rely on the ancient heritage of people and their stages of development. They depend on the collective memory of knowledge communication which constantly undergoes regular changes. Games reflect all forms of life in their communities. They also reflect the following: (1) the concepts associated with the community values (2) the relationship between the individual, his community, the others, and cultural heritage, (3) the culture of a community, and (4) the relationship between the community and nature. Thus, games are the mirror of all aspects of life.

Games are related to both performative and hand-made arts. They also give an outline of the features of the oral heritage of communities. For games usually incorporate elements of physical performance accompanied with the phonetic creativity associated with a specific poetic text. They might also depend on certain tools according to the nature of game.

My interest in games began since 1988 after my visit to the tombs of Kajmni and Morruka at Saqqara in Giza. These tombs date back to the sixth dynasty of ancient Egyptian state.

There are various forms of games painted on the walls of these tombs. Some of these games are still played in Upper Egypt. I, personally, practiced some of these games in my childhood. This caught my interest and encouraged me to trace the historic development of these games all over Egypt. Sooner, I visited Luxor in 1992. The very accurate creations of the young rural sculptor who enjoys his childhood silently amidst hard daily work held my attention. I began to study games in different areas in Egypt. For a long time, I spared no effort to hold sculptural and game workshops in South Egypt because of my love to this creative human experience.

There are many studies related to popular games in the fields of arts and education. These have been mainly research topics in the faculties of arts, education, physical education and musics. However, the most important one is a study by Prof. Dr. Lyla 'Allam which was under the supervision of the leading artist Saad Alkhadem.

I wish I could publish my full-length study on games which I have been working on for quite a long time ago. But many circumstances set that back. So, I decided to print it into parts featuring all that I hope to publish regarding the artistic athlete aspect of popular games. The publication is divided into parts according to subject.

Today, as I publish the first study in the field of popular games, I remember old women in my village and our games and laughs in the yards of our houses. I also remember walking and having fun and playing games along the banks of the river in my village. Popular games helped us more than anyone else to understand the nature of the Egyptian countryside and share all its authentic inherited values.

If we stand as demonstrators today in all Egyptian squares, it is because of the dreams of our childhood that taught us the love of the land and adherence to the values.

Playing, as an expression associated with human collective conscience, endorses love, self-confidence and trust in the universe. It is a contemplative worship and a broader belief in the Creator of the universe.

We are all humans. We all play. This is a motto of a phase that we should live on the athletic, artistic and social domains. Playing and pleasure influence many decisions in our daily life. They bring together many viewpoints among generations, cultures or different social classes.

We all play because we are all human beings.

Dr. Eman Mahran
Alharam, Giza, Egypt
November 2012

1

THE PHILOSOPHY OF POPULAR GAMES

THE PHILOSOPHY OF POPULAR GAMES

What are popular games?

Studies of popular games are known within the field of sport. However, studying popular games is not exclusively the specialty of the sports field. Popular games belong basically to the human popular heritage which is related to many aspects of the body.

The body is the most effective tool in games. Therefore, games are related to biology, psychiatry, sociology, fine arts, educational sciences, folkloric studies, and literature in its various forms. They can involve anyone who can exert efforts to benefit from the physical abilities of the body be him/her an actor in the theatre, cinema, semiotics arts or other fields of art.

We will try in the following lines to explore the nature of games from the viewpoint of folkloric culture.

First: Folkloric Culture as a Perspective:

Folkloric culture is the product of the 'common people'. Folkloric culture has its 'popular' characteristics because the common people are the ones who produce and consume it. The achievements of the popular culture are a 'collective' creation that belongs to the masses of the common people. It is not attributed to specific members. Folkloric cultures has its own methods and mechanisms which ensure that no cultural product spreads without the collective approval of the common people. Thus, no product is integrated in culture unless it fits their requirements and matches their continually renewed vision as new generations are born with new living conditions.[1]

1 'Abdulhamid Hawwas, Awraaq Fi Al-thaqafah Al-Sha'abeyyah. (Papers in Folkloric Culture). GEPO, 2006. p. 101

Ezickson pinpointed the traditional characteristics of folkloric culture stressing that folkloric culture is the same as the living traditional culture. With regard to the degree of difference in traditions from one culture to another, Ezikson states that the more primitive the culture is, the more traditional it becomes. Therefore, he describes folkloric culture as being basically 'traditional' when compared to a more advanced one.[2]

Mac Gregor also included, under the concept of 'heritage', the "deeply-rooted human characteristics and fixed trends and methods in the performance of things that are passed on from one generation to another". Gojn, who uses a more specific definition of cultural heritage, defines heritage as "a distinct way of lifestyle as reflected in various aspects of normal local culture and which is characterized throughout that period by an ongoing basic organic unity."[3]

The degree of traditionality varies obviously from one society to another. There is clear tendency to increase in traditionality in groups of farmers more than any other group because these simple groups adopt a simple stable lifestyle with little flexibility or change in their environment. Some people say that traditionalism is often accompanied with a conservative politician tendency.[4]

Because folkloric culture tend to be innovative, flexible and multi-sided, it must not be defined according to a specific intellectual orientation or a vision that is subject to historical or cultural factors.

Every region has its folkloric culture (at its time), and vision about its heritage which does depend on the importance of heritage but rather on the moment this heritage is appreciated. For example, the bride's chest (a piece of furniture to keep a bride's belongings) is differently appreciated and evaluated from one age to another, from one social level to another and from one artistic model to another. It is not an ordinary box. It is a cultural symbol that can be defined and re-defined according to every reader, his culture, his age and his social background.

The writer believes that defining folkloric culture has been largely and for a long time subject to the viewpoints of researchers in folkloric literature, legends and linguistics. Sooner it became the domain of interest of sociologists

2 Muhammad Al-Gohari, Dirasaat Fi 'Elm Al-folklore, (Studies in Folkloe). Dar 'Ain for studies and anthropological researches. (Quoted from Muhammad Al-Gohari et. al., Qamous Al-Ethnologia Wa Al-Folklore, (Dictionary of Ethnology and Folklore). p. 89

3 Ibid, p. 33

4 Ibid, 134, p. 7

and anthropologists. Now, it is the domain of men of art and material culture who support artists and creative people. Those will develop and make use of it in the age of picture. It will so easily be digitalized and promoted as ready-made products.

Second: Definition of Popular Games:

Here we will talk about popular games. We will start by the linguistic definition of 'games'. In Arabic, it is said:"*la'a'aba alsabi* he played with the boy, *tala'aba* manipulate/played *ol'obaan* ardent player *allo'ba* an object of play/game e. g. chess, toy pistols, a doll and so on.

When said *ragol lo'bah* this denotes a weak man, *Nawbat al-la'eb* is the turn in a game *leman al-lo'bah?* is an interrogative meaning "whose turn is it?" *faragha men lo'batoh* he finished the game. *Al-la'a'aab* the one whose job is playing such as the juggler and the monkey player. *La'oub* the person who plays a lot (playful). *Almal'ab* means the playground, the place of the game."[5]

The definitions of popular games has been handled mostly by scholars of physical education, arts and sociologists. Some of these will be briefly discussed.

Ali Hussein Qandeel states that "games and popular skills are considered an athlete heritage that has its own national history." He calls for gathering, recording and renewing it in order to keep it from being lost. Our popular games with the great skills they involve show our personality, our activeness and ambition, in the past and the present. They also aim to achieve training, readiness, movement and dominance either in thinking or at work. They seek to refine human instincts through singing and highlighting humane characteristics. In addition to being recreational, they ease the troubles and concerns of life. Finally, they are the product of our vitality because we always loathe laziness and lethargy and innately and naturally tend to increase vitality in all stages of life."[6]

Khalifa Ahmed[7] also stressed that the games are created by the people and are kept through ages by being taught and transferred from one generation to another."[8]

5 _____, *Al-MuheeT*. (Dictionary) Magma' al-lughah Al-'Arabeyyah. Vol. 2

6 Ahmad Al-Sabbahi Awad Khalil, *Al-Mahaarat Wa Al-Al'aab Al-Sha'abeyyah* (Skills and Popular Games). Dar Al-Kitaab al-'Arabi for publishing. N. D., p. 3

7 Khaleefah Ahmad Mohammad, *Al'aab Al-Šibyah Wa Al-Atfaal Fi Al-Sudaan*(Children and Teenagers Games, in The Sudan) GEBO, 2005.

8 Ibid, 1973

Ahmed Rushdi Saleh's definition of popular games is as follows, "any game spontaneously played by the common people from the cradle to the grave and inherited from generation to another. People may change or modify them sometimes; however both women and men equally play them as early as their childhood."[9]

Kamal Eldeen Hussein defines them as "spontaneous games which are simple in their organization and performance. They do not require playgrounds or equipments. They are played inside rooms and in yards. They just require the desire to play on part of the child and some simple tools of the environment. If the child's body itself is not the tool, then they use parts of plants. . a palm leave, a log or a fruit."[10]

According to the classification proposed by Mohammed Al-Gohary popular games are included under the heading of folkloric arts and material culture which is the fourth branch of folklore's tree diagram. The writer disagrees with this classification because it is based on the categorization of a school of sociology.

The writer believes that popular games incorporate both physical and non-physical elements. However, they are essentially related to the physical category because of the association of the body in all its creations within this field. They also follow the non-physical category because of their literary texts and intellectual content which is representative of various lifestyles of the environment.

In this book, popular games denote the innovative arts based on participation. Those games trigger and produce thought, movement or performance. They are not confined in place or ruled by an organizational body. They rather depend on simple and easy rules and conditions which facilitate handling them and guarantee a fast geographic popularity. There are no conditions to play them regarding gender or age. Therefore, games are considered an outlet that allows a wide-range social participation. They match, in their diversity, the early development of humans because of their association with the sensual nature and the physical and mental growth of the human beings.

9 Al-Al'aab Al-Sha'beyyah Wa Al-Maharaat Al-Gesmeyyah Wa Al-Sirk(Popular Games, Physical Skills and The Circus) Magllat Al-Finoun Al-Sha'beyyah (Folkloric Arts Magazine). Vol. 24, p. 74. GEBO, Cairo, 1988
10 Kamaal El-Din Hussein, *Al-'Aab Al-ATfaal Al-Ghinaaeyyah* (Melodic Games of Children) Dar Al-Fikr Al-'Arabi, Cairo, 1991

Games are a traditional flexible heritage that carries the features of creativity because they depend on originality and innovation as well.

The player is not the only owner of these creations. All the surroundings may add to or remove from the game. The game is a collective creation related to its environment.

Games are a collective accumulative legendary legacy bearing the remnants of the times when both the body and symbolic formation were the basis of human communication.

Games and the Natural Environment

Games are the product of nature. They are a means of getting in harmony with it whether for the young or old player. It represents a positive interaction with the creatures that surround the human being.

The environment contributes to training the player on flexibility, movement and playing. It offers him many cultural inputs that allow him to deal with those who surround him. Friends ,spaces and the available material play a role in determining the pattern of the games a player might play.

Environments vary in a way that influences the features of everyday life such as:

*The agricultural environment: This environment is characterized by the existence of dark alluvium that can be simply formed and burned in the countryside. This is why land, plants and agricultural systems give the farmer a lot of information about the arts of agriculture in ancient times. The child here is knowledged with plant and botanic products or distinctive remains such as dry stems that can be either used or recycled. Also, there are games associated with specific agricultural seasons such as harvest times and floods.

*The coastal environment: This environment grants children freedom and a sense of space. Here, the child feels his body an item of the place. It also surrounds him with sand, salt, sea creatures, shells, etc. This environment allows its inhabitants air, water and sand. Thus, ball games and sand formations are among the most popular games played by the children.

*The desert environment: It is characterized by the wide areas, stones, dunes which propel thinking and meditation. The most famous games there depend on palms, stones and other materials in the desert environment.

The Importance of Popular Games

Popular games are among the oldest forms of human activity. They are the first form of human activity in childhood. They echo man's emotions and show his pleasures and happiness. They reflect the image of life. They thrived over ages and are common to various peoples. Every nations has its own games. Games display the form of life in the environment with its own characteristics, traditions and systems.[11]

Popular games play a role in transferring the cultural heritage of society to the child. They ingrain in him specific social values which train the child on building social relationships and dealing with others. This develops his social interaction and teaches him the importance of living within a group and keeping away from individualism and isolationism.[12]

Introduction to the Study of Popular Games

When studying popular games, we rely on classifications. Popular games are classified according to the stages of the game, its end and its goal. Is its goal mental (intellectual)? Physical (motor)? Or imaginative?

We can say that games are generally classified according to physical fitness, mental ability, and age group.

The scientific classifications on which studying the popular games depends on are numerous. Following are examples of these classifications:

First classification:
- Form of game (intellectual or physical).
- Type of game (competitive or fun games).
- Formation (simple or complex games).
- Age groups (games for children, teens (girls, boys) or adult games).
- Number of players (individual, pairs or team games).[13]

11 Mohammad 'Adel Khattab, *Al-Al'aab Al-Reefeyyah Al-Sha'beyyah*(Rural Popular Games). The Anglo-Egyptian Bookshop, 1964

12 Waheeb Mohammad Labeeb, *Al-Al'aab Al-Sha'beyyah Wa Dawrohah Fi Tansheat Al-Tefl Fi Al-Marhalah Al-Senneyyah Min (6-12) Sanah: Dirashah Maydaneyyah Liba'Ḍ Qura Muhafazat Al-Sharqehyyqueah*(Popular Games and Their Role in Upbringing Children in The Age Group (6-12) years: A Survey Study of Some Villages in Sharqyyah Governorate)Ph. D Thesis The High Institute of Theatre, Art Academy, Cairo, 1998

13 Ibid, p. 10

Second classification:

• First: Quiet games (non-physical/static) such as solving puzzles, paper games and so on.

• Second: Physical games: These are divided into three sub-categories:

- Small games: They are easy simply-organized games. They do not require great physical skills. There are no fixed or specific regulations to govern them.

- Elementary games: They represent an advanced stage over small games where the physical skills acquired from small simple games are developed into motor skills that prepare the player for team games such as basketball, volleyball, handball, football and other games.

- Big games: These are team games. They also include all the physical activities performed using the ball as a tool. There are also the games characterized by the competitiveness which necessitates a high level of performance. These are performed in the form of collective competitions (team games), pair games or individual games. These games are held in accordance to international rules and laws which determine the time of the game, number of players, the playground area, tools of the game, method of playing and rules. . . etc.[14]

The writer believes that games can be classified as follows:

- Intellectual games (these depend on mental abilities)
- Physical games (They are the performative games such as singing, dancing, acting, etc.)
- Realia (Three-dimensional games) (toys and objects)
- Verbal games (songs, riddles and others)

Popular Games as a Viewpoint of Reading Human History

Human History is constituted from ages with various concepts. Despite having common aspects, these ages are so variant that we assert the importance of adopting the viewpoint of reading and interpreting legacy through a symbolic and semiotic perspective of games. Games are a stage in human development. Partnership in creating human history at interrelated regions

---

14 Mohammad Ahmad Abdullah Ibrahim, *Madkhal Fi Al-Al'aab Al-Šagheerah* (An Introduction to Small Games). Al-Mutahidoon LilTeba'ah, Zagazig, 2005

and between cultures and areas all over the ancient world had its influence on drawing an outline of the ancient world and the items and tools at play in games then.

Games draw a complex movement rather than an abstract one. We have to read these signs which could chronicle and record for an occupation, a festival or a bitter criticism of the regime.

The game is an expression of meaning and an outlet equal to, but simpler than, seriousness. It also guarantees continuity because it transcends over a possible dramatic event to the sarcastic impossible comic.

The meaning and significance of every finger, palm or foot movement could be a rooted in an old belief or in a pagan ritual of antique ages. We have to start relating to each other. These games are "the residues in the long-awaken, fatigued body of humanity"

Games and Performative Arts

Performative arts here refer to the various arts related to body movement, where the player tries to play roles within a pre-set consensual scenario. These roles range within a number of imitations of the public patterns of individuals surrounding him. They pinpoint the child's experience towards others. In imitating his grandparents and parents, the child presents an emotional and critical performance of the social functions he perceives. Following is a script for a theatrical game where a group of children stand in row in front of one child who is symbolically named "The Sultan", "The Jinni", "The Magician", "The Minister", etc. The child of position moves to and fro and keeps singing. Once the rest of the children shout "Run and catch him", they all start running and he chases them till he catches one to join him. The game goes on till he catches everyone. The last one to catch is the one to be 'The Sultan' or whatever position once the game starts over.

Following is the song of the game[15]:

Child	: Boom ... boom ... boom
Child	: Boom ... boom ... boom
Group	: Who? Who? Who?
Group	: I am the Sultan (Jinni or magician, etc.)

---

15 Baheegah Rasheed, Ibid, p. 67

Child   : I want Sami (or Adel or Sara, … any child's name)
Group   : Run and catch him/her

Children play with various media. They sing, paint and deal with birds and pets. They listen to interesting fairy-tales and perform symbolic series. Their life is built on learning and activity. Though the education they get at that stage it is not a written and documentary as happens later at advanced ages.

Children learn about life through life, eventually gain positive and correct habits, attitudes, information and concepts.[16]

Games as the Child's Private Theater

Games are the oldest theatrical script on earth. The child as a critic and an actor adopts the stance of the viewer to his dreams. He writes the script and gives roles but at the end he seeks nothing but pleasure.

This form of play could mean him a lot because through it the child expresses his opinion and also establishes his expressive creative space that asserts his existence among his human group. Therefore, games are the deepest form of criticism and the truest creative performative image deviced by the human mind.

Child's play should be incorporated among the circles of free uncensored,unretributed expression. The child is free to live the circumstances of his age. Imitation, criticism and revealing both advantages and disadvantages are all issues related to games.

Games are not mere laughs, movements or songs. They provide serious criticism of that which the child experiences in his natural environment.

First Games in History

Man in stone ages resorted to magic for fear of death and hunger and to protect himself against the attacks of his enemies. When he started growing plants and raising cattle he discovered that his life depended on the weather good or bad, rain, sunshine, lightening snow, plagues, famines, land fertility and abundant marrows or their scarcity. "This feeling accompanied the idea of jinnis and spirits of all kinds and the good and evil spirits which

16 Mahmoud Al-Basuiony, *Rosoum Al-ATfaal Qabl Al-Madrasah* (Pre-school Children Paintings). Dar Al-Ma'aref, Cairo, 1991, p. 105

provide blessings or inflict plagues. It also accompanied other ideas such as the unknown, the mysterious and the supreme powers towards which man is helpless. Hence, appeared spiritual worships and belief in self-continuity and worshipping the dead. This raised the need to have idols, tarots, symbols, sacrifices, vow gifts, tomb charities and cemeteries."[17]

With the imitation of nature at that time[18] (early primitive ages), dolls were created where we find an attempt at the simplification and abstraction to some extent of the general shape in a way that simulates nature but is not identical to it. Moreover, some animals, plants and geometrical decorations were added to some of these dolls which mostly carried totemic magic symbols. Saad Al-Khadem says, "There are rituals and habits that lived ever since the dawn of humanity. These have mingled with religion, magic and the imagination of primitive man and even became part of the superstitions he engulfed himself with. These habits and rituals, despite their weirdness and illogicality, entrenched in him perseverance, forbearance, cleverness and various other skills in hope for getting rid of the influence of the evil spirits he fears. He also hoped to control these spirits and tame them into serving him. Eventually, man ended up discovering large horizons of many artifacts, arts and industries.

Muhammad Anwar Shokr states that some of the dolls dating back to primitive ages are made of clay and pottery. These are shaped in the form of naked women with very simple and primitive carvings of the feminine body. However, one of these is a small statue of a woman in fine carvings and sensitive lines. It attests for the craftsmanship of the sculptor and his good observation at that historic age.[19]

It is difficult to accurately trace the origin of games and toys and their history. Games were known ever since the first ages of humanity. Stones, pebbles and branches of trees and animal bones were used as tools for games.

Primitive man watched monkeys and other animals grab twigs and branches and swing in the air from one tree to another. The tree is the first swing in history. Man then used animal skins to make drums and made flutes as toys. No doubt singing is the oldest art. It is known since the beginning of

17 Arnold Howards, *Art and Society in History*. Dar Al-Kitaab al-'Arabi for Publishing, Cairo. N. D. , p. 26

18 Saad Al-khadem, *Al-Fan Al-Sha'abi Wa Al-Mo'ataqadat Al-Sehreyyah*(Folkloric Art and Magical Beliefs). Maktabat Al-NahĎah, Cairo, N. D. , p. 26

19 Mohammad Anwar Shokri, *Al-Fan Al-MeŠri Al-QaĎeemian* (Ancient Egypt Art) Al-Muasassah Al-MeŠreyyah Al-'Ammah for Writing and Publishing, Cairo, N. D.

history. It is natural for all people for it is a means of expressing the motions man experiences all through his life. For example, children in early age sometimes sing innovative tunes while playing. Some primitive tribes living in the outskirts in Australia do not have any kind of musical instruments , yet their songs are characterized with regular rhythm and systematic tempo.[20]

Dolls in their various forms are tangible material art in the space. They take the shape of the living creature be it an animal or a human being. Man employs the materials of the environment surrounding him to create dolls in any available technology. Dolls can be made by the hands of a craftsman or an ordinary person. They are take the shape of lovable and holy creatures be it an animal, a person, a bird ... etc.

Yulis Leebis states that all people of the world invented the cutest and funniest toys to enrich and embellish the early years of the lives of their offsprings in a joyful educational manner. Parents make dolls and toys and all the tools pertaining to a happy childhood.

The toys of the Egyptian civilization are provided for example, with movable limbs that are highly realistic. Some of these dolls have wigs of human-hairs with tiny clay balls at the end of the hair as do contemporary Nubian girls in Upper Egypt. The only difference is that balls at the end of Nubian girls are made of grease rather than clay.

Old Egyptians provided their young daughters with mini-houses highly-furnished with tiny models of furniture and linen as used by adults. We could find a mini-mirror at the wall and even draws in the cupboard. The funniest examples are the animal toys of old Egypt, Babel and Aššur. These animals were in the shape of an alligator with movable jaw or a hog, etc. They would be fixed to a cart and drawn with a string. Other real pets and tame animals were raised to play with the children e.g. birds, monkeys and hoopoe which was well-loved because of the colored crown at his head.[21]

20 Baheegah Rasheed, *Aghani Wa Al'aab Sha'abeyyah lilaTfaal* (Popular Songs and Games for Children). 'Aalam Alkutub, 1976.
21 Yuluis Leebes, *AŠl Al-Ashyaa:Bedayaat Al-Thaqafah Al-Insaneyyah* (The Origin of Things:The Beginnings of Human Culture) Translator: Kamel Ismail, Damascus, Dar Al-Mada for Culture and Publishing, 1988

Symbols and Games

A symbol, 'ramz', in **Lisaan Alarab Dictionary** is "an unvoiced movement of the tongue. It is done either through moving the lips in undistinguished movements with no voice"[22]. Accordingly, the author thinks that *ramz* here denotes exclusively miming signs/symbols.

Matn Allughah Dictionary gives the definition of a sign/symbol as follows: "*ramaza, yarmazu, ramzan* i.e. to sign, or mime using lips, eyes, eyebrows or any possible object"[23]. This definition refers to 'motor' symbols done through moving parts of the face and attracting attention to a specific object.

Alm'ugam AlmuħeeT states that "many poets use rain as a symbol for giving and blessings."[24]

Symbols/signs are referred to in the Glorious Quran, e.g.:

"كَتَّبَّرِ رُكُذْاَو اَزْمَرّ ّالإِمْآيَأَ قَثَالَثْ سَأْنِنَالَ مَلَكُتْ ّالَاَ كُتَيَ ّالَقاَ ّيّلَ لَ عُجَجاربَرَ لَقاَ''
 كَ ثْيِرَ اَرَ وَسَبَّحْ ّبِالإِعَشَيِّوَاّلإِبْكْآرَ رِ ''آيةِ 41 سوررة لَ عمران''

He said, "My Lord, make for me a sign." He Said, "Your sign is that you will not [be able to] speak to the people for three days except by gesture. And remember your Lord much and exalt [Him with praise] in the evening and the morning." Verse 41,surrat Al-'imran[25]

"A sign/symbol is an object that indispensible to refer to something."[26] This definition states that a sign/symbol is a tool of reference for an object. It stands for that 'another' so that the relation between them is that of the private to the public or the material to the abstract. A symbol is material; however, it might refer to an idea or a specific meaning. For example, pigeon is a symbol of peace, the cross of Christianity. Some movements could also be used as symbols e. g. moving the palm of hand to seek quietness and calmness.[27]

André Gabr has an idiosyncratic opinion in symbols/signs. He states that truths remain hidden behind symbols.[28]

22 _____, Lisaan Al'Arab (Lisaan Al'Arab Dictionary), p. 256

23 _____, Matn Allughah (The Explantion of Language), p. 647

24 _____, Al-MuheeT. (Dictionary) Magma' al-lughah Al-'Arabeyyah. Vol. 2, p. 631

25 The Glorious Quran

26 Philip Spring, *Al-Ramzeyyah Fi Loghat Al-Adyaan Wa Al-Hayah* (Symolism in Life and Liturgical Language). Translated in Damascus, 1992, p. 41

27 Ibid, p. 5

28 Ibid, p. 499

Symbols are related to art and its purity. Some defined symbolism as the art of expressing and referring to ideas by re-incarnating them in the minds of readers through unexplained signs/symbols.[29]

Mohsen Attyah states that a "symbol is a form of reference used because of the denotational link between it and its reference."[30] He also states that symbolism was essentially used to hide holy truths from the secularist. These truths would be interpreted and realized only by those who can decipher these symbols. No sooner these truths are represented in symbols, than their transferability depends on the capacity of the mind to understand them. Hence, symbols were used in ancient civilizations and are still used up till now.[31]

The author states that there is a variation in symbols; their secrets and meanings. This is the case in visual symbols be they painted or sculptured and also in motor and verbal symbols be they movements of the whole body signs or of specific organs used to denote a specific idea. In all these forms of symbols there is a material representation of an idea or of another object.

Symbols are differently used from one place to another, from one age to another and from a group of users to others. The local community has its say in the connotations of symbols. This is very evident in clothes, forms, jewelry, hand signs, voices etc. Symbols can be classified into political, religious and social ones.

There are symbols which denote forms or the philosophy and meanings of these forms. There are also symbols which relate to the senses and their capacities to refer and express. As early as man could carve his artistic experiences in caves and on rocks, symbolism accompanied these experiences. It then developed to distinguish and incarnate various cultures in plastic arts and various other symbolisms.

The symbolic attitude for the child is a crystallization of schemes; an accumulation bearing explicit visual connotations. Symbolism fits the referent intellectually, emotionally, socially and aesthetically. Intellectually, a symbol

29 Gabr Ibrahim Gabr, *Al-Ostoorah Wa Al-Ramz; Mabadi Naqdeyyah Wa TaTbiqaat:Khams 'Ashr Dirasah liKham 'Ashr Naqid* (Myth and the Symbol; Critical Principles and Applications: Fifteen Studies by Fifteen Authors). Baghdad, 1973, p. 6

Mohsen Atteyah, Al-Fan Wa 'Aalam Al-Ramz(Art and The world of Symbols) Dar Al-Ma'aref, Cairo, 1993, p. 58

30 Mohsen Atteyah, *Al-Fan Wa 'Aalam Al-Ramz*(Art and The world of Symbols) Dar Al-Ma'aref, Cairo, 1993, p. 58

31 Ibid, p. 48

is a mental process which establishes relations and conceptual ideas that pinpoints the child's status in the intellectual movement.

Emotionally, a symbol is chosen by the child to express his feelings of strength, weakness, courage, affectation, assertion and hesitation. All these variant feelings give vitality to symbols and render them vibrant and expressive of the human psyche. Socially, a symbol is the production of society's interactions. It carries various connotations that accurately portray the society.[32]

Symbolic Connotations of Games

Games have various forms. They bear philosophical contents and symbolisms. Games are played in an environment of particular beliefs and symbols upon which concepts and values are based. Accordingly, games are an explicit theatrical and performative reflection of these concepts.

The movements performed in games might have social, religious, sensual and even sexual connotations. Games are the product of both the human body and culture as well.

Games as the Issue of the Body

The body is related to games. They are its main medium of expression. Mental capacities in combination with physical abilities work to harmoniously to enact a concordance upon which the body's creativity is based.

Games are the formal production of the body which enables it to live in harmony with the surrounding universe. Games are closely related to the body and its control abilities amidst all the stimuli surrounding and propelling it into motor expression.

Symbols and Physical Art

Physical art is dependent on the potentialities of the body, its curves and artistic abilities. It is also subject to the vision of the owner of that body. This vision is subject, in turn, to the system of values of the society which could grant him freedom at an early age leading to an increase in the symbols related to it.

32 Mahmoud Al-Basuiony, ibid, p. 114

Symbols are associated with free flexible body arts. Those body arts employ a wide and suggestive range of creativities of that wondrous creature: man. People create and use thousands of signs and symbols as used in semiotics and sign language. Daily new cultural innovations are born. However, the body keeps a pioneer position in the symbolic vision of man. The mental powers of man put the body into action and push it to excel in using its limited powers into supremacy.

The Body as an Artistic Unit

The body should be handled as an artistic unit of integrated details. This artistic unit is included in a highly-complex universal formation that allows it a space for movement and harmony with its context. Basically, the body is a sculpture. Artistically, it is the object of aesthetics and communication between man and nature.

Mother-child play is an explicit beginning of the relationship between one body and another. Hers is not like any other. Her body is the universe for that child. It provides him with love, containment and social security. Therefore, the mother's songs and her touches and the depth of her responses and physical interaction with the child influence his attitude and love for life. This directly shows in his immediate relations with his peers, his approach to play and his self-assertion in environment. It is a communicative relation between two lumps. Later, this is embodied in his sexual and natural practices of life. The body is a single unit of positive interactional characteristics surrounded by other material units.

Various Factors Affecting Popular Games

There are various influences affect the form and nature of popular games. These are:

- Place: The geographic dimension which determines the weather, the nature of the human gatherings and its level of development. It also controls the available environmental material.
- Time: It defines the phase the society lives; the totality of freedom practices allowed at that historic period and the development of civilization in that society.

- Economic conditions: Economy plays an important role in the life of the individual, supplying his needs and affecting his affordance to toys and accessibility to game practices.
- Social concepts: These refer to customs and traditions.
- Cultural background: Upon which the individual builds his knowledge of society and communicational information and also his sense of belonging.
- Religious beliefs: These directly define the limitations and freedom practices of the child. They determine the level of symbolism used and provide the onset to his relation and interaction with others.
- Cultural dimension and the individual's accumulated idiosyncratic game experiences.
- The space yards available for games and play.
- Commerce and exchange relations between people.
- Human interactions and the relation networks of the society itself. Some societies are open and others are closed.
- The abilities of the folkloric artist and his creative formation of tools and games.
- The availability of environmental materials.

Places for Games and Play

Games are mostly played at houses, yards (indoors or open one), river banks or under trees and palms. They could also be played in parks, clubs, cafes or open spaces . All places are fit for traditional games.

2

THE PSYCHOLOGICAL AND EDUCATIONAL ASPECTS OF POPULAR GAMES

THE PSYCHOLOGICAL AND EDUCATIONAL ASPECTS OF POPULAR GAMES

In this chapter we will focus on the importance of playing for the child and its role in his growth and character formation.

Makaritko states that playing for the child is as important as working/ having a job for the adult. The way a child acts in his play, the way he largely becomes in his job. A child's character is largely formed very early during his play. Consequently, preparing the child for the future should never be based on the exclusion of play from his childhood and life .It should be incorporated in such a systematized way that strengthens the physical abilities of the child in his growth.[33]

For example, the child-doll friendship is one of the deepest of its kind. The child deals with the doll as an independent creature which shares his life, dreams and future. Consequently, it distinctively shapes his relationships with his peers.

Games develop various abilities for the child; physical and mental. <u>On the mental domain, games help the following</u>:

*Developing attention and concentration

*Developing expectation and intuition

*Developing senses

*Developing the creative abilities and manual crafts skills

33 Viola Albiblawy,*Magallat 'Alam Al-Fikr* (The World of Intellect). Kuwait, vol. 10, 3rd ed., 1979

<u>As for the physical skills, games help the following</u>:
*Positively letting out the physical energy
*Discovering talented children to increase their potentialities
*Pinpointing aspects of strength and weakness in the child to develop them
*Achieving a proper physical growth
*Achieving a state of psychological balance between the child and his peers

Human Creativity in Games

Creativity is the most supreme mental ability that matches the individual's ability to use his skills. Games, in this respect provide a wonderous variety of attractions. They are a means of access both to the authentic and the amazing and imaginarily new. Hence, they help in creating a state of balance between creativity and authenticity.

Games carry enough symbolism to be a direct representation of local culture. They are also dependent on the cultural context which directly affects creativity in them. This is evident in the following contextual factors:

*Weather: It has various elements (coldness, dryness, heat, wind, etc.) which are key players in determining the nature of garments and clothes worn in society.

*Local material: refer to the materials the player finds available to use and create with. These are influenced by the environmental conditions and the variety of forms the environment provides. The environment is the main agent in culture and variation. The environment sharpens the craftsmanship of the creator through the materials it supplies or variation in them, etc.

*Economic Situation: refers to the financial state of the society of the player which directly affects the form and type of the game/play product and the time permitted for these games.

Games as a Critical Concept: The Child as a Model

Some societies practice the limitation and confinement of the child's movement aiming to discipline him and control his movement so that he would fit to live in his community. The child, on the other hand, continually produces direct impulsive critical reactions .Impulsive reactions for the child are not just a form of expression; they are tools of confrontation and conveying a critical the content as felt by the child.

Playing and games are effective tools of criticism, they are reflected in an expressive artistic frame whether by imitation, dancing or acting mini-dramas that have scenarios, symbols, and vocabulary related to the criticized topic.

Criticism is built on observation and scrutiny. It is a proof of freedom and evidence on the doors open for one child which might not be accessible to another. The child's attempts to create and show proof of his existence and to leave his own creations are driven either by his wild imagination or by his ignorance of the societal complexities surrounding him.

The environment entrenches over control, dictatorship and repression of the child's imagination. Environments are similarly governed by norms and traditions which over dominate those in society.

Games create a balance between the child's needs and the wishes of community. They give a reading and interpretation of the concepts influencing the child. The child is always truthful in his feelings and a representative speaker of his society. His vision, despite young age, is deeper and more truthful. He has no underlying interests and is not well-aware of the confinements of society, hence his honest criticism.

Games, then, are an evident well-established recreational and motor outlet of lexical meanings. They convey a message to those who surround the child. Although games are a means in themselves, they have an essential target which is moving with the child from the stage of the imaginary and unreal he experiences amidst his surroundings into the stage of discerning reality and having a direct interaction with an evident role in his human community.

Popular Games and Their Role in Social Development

Games are beneficial to the individual. They are part of the basic factors of modern life. An individual who plays is healthier and more balanced than those who are deprived from recreation. Games affect physical and mental health as well as morals which govern the roles of play. They diminish crime and work into various ways for the integration of society.

Popular games achieve social satisfaction and concordance because they realize[34]:

- Equality.
- Tolerance.
- Criticism of society.

34 Waheeb Mohammad Labeeb, ibid, p. 172

- Discovering talents and employing them.
- Freedom.
- Sense of belonging.
- Steadiness and willpower.
- Honesty.
- Preparing and setting for a social role.

The importance of games and playing is that they represent a normal attitude that propels the player to express himself and realize happiness and pleasure. This urges man to work more. Games also constitute a wealth of experiences and provide effective natural exercises for the mind and senses which help forming and developing a strong character. Moreover, they strengthen the body and improve health and mental growth. They also provide chances for social change and moral re-assessment. Through games the society achieves welfare. They consolidate elegant human relations and enjoyable deep friendship which creates harmony and unity.[35]

Solomon states that games are important for the following reasons[36]:

1. They help the child release his anxieties and repressed aggression towards his father or brothers.
2. They eliminate feelings of guilt.
3. They provide a good opportunity to freely express all the lovable fancies of the child.
4. Games incorporate all possible therapies of growth.
5. Games eliminating phobias and sensitivities through repetition.

Games are a useful tool for social development because of the following:

1. They help achieve communication with the surrounding environment,promoting work with individuals in it and consolidating group spirit.
2. Developing social relations and the sense of belonging for society and place.

Games affect the child's character and his upbringing socially, culturally, psychologically and physically. A study categorized the relationship between games and children as follows[37]:

1. There are games which aim to teach and bring up children to think, expect, behave well and develop their senses.

35 Mohammad 'Adel Khattab, ibid, pp. 15-16
36 Mohammad Ahmad Abdullah Ibrahim, ibid, p. 25
37 Waheeb Mohammad Labeeb, ibid.

2. Games which teach children adaptation to the environment, its animals and modern means of transportation.

3. Games which teach children the skills of physical sports and develop group spirit, competition and taking initiatives.

4. Games which teach children role-playing, and to have sense of belonging and be socially integrated.

5. Games which teach children to develop their manual abilities and creation.

The study revealed that children in various age groups pass various stages of development from simple to complex. They try through observation and imitation with their elderly in play to role-play them.

They practice games and even partly join them. As soon as they perfect the game and its techniques they are readily invited to play. Thus games are passed on from one generation to the other through direction and imitation[38].

Benefits of Games

The benefits of games and playing are the following:

- Games help the child express himself, discover his personality and enrich his character. They help develop the speech of the child and enable him to learn and perfect many motor skills.

- Games highlight gender characteristics. Boys tend to practice violent games that show their physical strength whereas girls tend to choose team games and rhythm activities. The teenager is more successful in breaching the gap between childhood and adulthood if he could practice several sports in an average skill.

- Games are also important for adults. Despite old age they help improve movement, thinking abilities and emotions[39].

We can sum up the functions of games as follows:

- Individual function: Games increase the agility, vitality, mental awareness and psychological health of the child. The child becomes more reliable and his will of power increases though playing. He is also trained on self-control, determination, perseverance and self-discipline which is the most supreme form of will of power.

38 Waheeb Mohammad Labeeb, ibid, p. 172
39 Mohammad Ahmad Abdullah Ibrahim, ibid, pp. 18-19

- Social function: Games entrench in the individual morals and virtues. It teaches him the importance discipline, respecting the rights of others and working to make them happy. They strengthen social ties, advocate cooperation and sacrificing for society welfare. Moreover, it ingrains chivalry and altruism which are the pillars of social reform.[40]

Theories of Games

Many sociologists and philosophers studied the underlying origins and motives for playing games and their various types. The similarities between games in various countries were also studied. Many theories have been set to account for games in their various forms. Some of prominent theories are the following[41]:

1) Surplus Energy theory:

The English philosopher Herbert Snibber in his **book Principles of Psychology** introduced what is now known as theory of surplus energy in games." This theory is built on the idea that children play in order to let out an excess of energy in their bodies. The body spends energy in its growth; if this energy reaches a maximal level, it would affect the nerves and generate involuntary movements. Games are necessary to release the surplus energy of the child.

2) Legacy theory:

Stanely Hall asserts that "playing and games are indispensible part of every individual's legacy. Games are passed on from one generation to another. . . Modern games are developed versions of old ones. . Games reflect the development of humanity. They embody that which the child inherited from his grandparents and portray the human phases of development from primitiveness into civilization. Children games show the roles man has undertaken to earn his living and support himself.

3)Bio-genetic theory:

Carl Bazel, the philosophy professor in Bazel in Switzerland, set this theory. He had an interest in studying games and was one of the pioneers who raised doubts about the fact that accepted characteristics could be inherited. Consequently, he laid his theory and explanations on principle of natural selection set by Darwin as one of the main factors of development. He also

40 Mohammad ʿAdel Khattab, ibid, pp. 16-17
41 Mohammad Ahmad Abdullah Ibrahim, ibid, pp. 20, 21, 22.

explained that games represent a common tendency to practice instincts and are deeply related to imitation which is another common instinct replacing a large number of stative instincts. Accordingly, games are a natural phenomenon of development and are considered part of the general disposition of man.

4) Recreation theory:

This theory is based on the fact that games and activities are practiced in leisure time by adults. Games for them are practiced to refresh their body from fatigue. Goots Mootsi emphasizes the recreational value of playing in eliminating nervous stress, mental fatigue and psychological anxieties. They are also important to refresh the body and re-vitalize it after long hours of work.

5) Self-expression Theory:

Mason asserts that man is an active creature; however, his physiological anatomy restricts his activities. Moreover, the agility of his body affects the types of activities he can practice. His physiological needs affect his psychological propensities which in turn determine the patterns of play and games he practices.

6) Social communication theory:

This theory states that man picks up the patterns of activities he finds common at home and in his society. Modernly, an attempt has been made to study the practices of upbringing a child. It has been found that physical skill games are common in societies which emphasize on success and achievement as the most important goals for children. Games are imitations of the society's main activities.

Functional Theory of Games

The author states that there is a direct relation between games and the physical buildup of the child at various ages.

Games are directly influenced by this buildup .The physical abilities of the child determine the details of the game and his need to move. The body and its creative abilities are the child's main tool of play. Consequently, the abilities of the body form and produce this creative physical and motor vision.

There is a direct relation between the body and the form of the game and its development. Every muscle plays a role in the accuracy and agility of the player in the game. The more grown up and perfect his growth , the larger is the number of details. Observation is an par essential part in this function.

Growth here is conditional to many factors. It depends on gene and the environment with many minor details, some of which are constant and the others are changeable.

Creativity and the mental artistic abilities are God-given talents. However, they can be positively employed in physical performance at games. Accordingly, games proportionally promote growth.

They prove that the player reached specific level of growth in the physical, mental and psychological abilities that is displayed in the total performance of the player in the games he plays. Therefore, physicians should take interest in games because we need a parallel physiological reading that understands the biological needs of the body of the player and links playing to its proper age group.

Playing is a physical outlet of growth. It is also a positive outlet of creative energy. It is a form of the body's direct relation with the environment. Games display the feelings towards the environment, the enjoyment and harmony of being part of it.

Age Groups of Games

Each age group has its specific games as related to age, gender, the social level and cultural background. Females and males share some childhood games. However, each gender has particular games that fit its physical abilities and social circumstances. There are also the recreational games which takes up the time of old people at an age when they no longer work and need to pass time peacefully and enjoyably.

Psychological Impact of Games on Children

Children grow up following nature's law; each in a particular way, governed by specific hereditary patterns and environmental inputs that result in individual idiosyncratic differences.

Genes affect the shape, style and behavior of an individual, and the environment either entrenches these qualities or wiping them away.

Games give[42] the child "the growth experiences necessary for deeper understanding and wisdom. They are experimental attempts to understand the nature of things and their characteristics. Every object the child lays hands on is subject to scrutiny and formation to find out its hidden aspects".

42 Mahmoud Al-Basuiony, ibid, p. 98.

<u>The child is influenced by the practices of the game. Games have a positive effect on him in the following:</u>

- Achieving psychological balance and increasing confidence in others and in himself.
- Emphasizing self-realization of the child in a group.
- Developing his mental and creative abilities.
- Developing and asserting his social abilities and positive behavior with others.
- Teaching the child numerous concepts, attitudes, habits and new pieces of information.
- Giving the child an opportunity to depend on himself and handle responsibility.

Advantages of Games

Games have several advantages. These are the following:

1) Games are a target:

Games are not a distinct pattern or a specific stereotyped energy. Games are dominated by the existence of special trends in behavior and by a particular general target of the energy or activity. Accordingly, every action in the game is graded as to its closeness of the target.

2) Games are impulsive:

Games are an impulsive activity, whereas work is obligatory and necessitates complying with the outside world. This raises the question whether elementary or even scientific thinking is less primitive than games? Or that they primarily lack impulsiveness? How, then, can we understand the impulsiveness of the artist in his production?

Games are an innerly-driven representation of the outside world whereas serious work is a representational process that targets balance and harmony with individuals or the environment. It has an external stimulus.

3) Enjoyment is the target of Games:

Games are activities that achieve pleasure whereas serious work is directed towards a beneficial goal regardless of its being enjoyable or not.

4) Games are not systematic:

Games lack organized formation. They contradict serious thinking which is characterized by accuracy and organization. Freud gives a noteworthy comment hereon analyzing games within the framework of his theory of the symbolism of the sub-conscious. He states that imaginative and symbolic games are not goal-oriented whereas logical thinking is harmonious, organized and goal-oriented. His explanation here is that symbolic games are not goal-oriented because the sub-conscious absorbs the outside reality, frees it from compliance to the general rules and then intertwines it with the subconscious desires. Thus games and play are not subject to logic, organization or orientation just like any subconscious phenomenon.

5) Games provide an outlet for psychological conflict:

Games do not involve psychological conflict. Conflicts are strange for game yards. Even if it shows up in that field, the self is sooner relieved from it through compensation, catharsis or free expression. On the other hand, the domain of serious work is filled with many unavoidable factors of psychological conflict.

No doubt this analysis is logical because it displays the discrepancy between freedom and obedience, submission and revolution. However, we should not forget that it is based on one aspect of the whole picture. In games, the inner self is in control; there are no conflicts whereas at work there is submission to reality with all its criteria, rules and judgments.

6) The social dimension of games:

Socially, games are a means through which children discover their hidden abilities and potentialities and hence become socially and culturally fostered in an appropriate way. In games, children gain a proper share of information particularly those relating to the environment of the game and its tools and circumstances. Thus games play a part of forming the conceptual and cognitive character of the child.[43]

Characteristics of Popular Games

Popular games are:
1. Simple so that they would easily spread out.
2. Learnable and of a transferrable knowledge content.
3. Symbolic and related to societal values.
4. Having a vocal expression concurrent with the body movement.

The Social Function of Songs Related to Games

The songs related to popular games are mainly vocalities unaccompanied by any musical or rhythmical instrument. They are not accompanied by

43 Mohammad Ahmad Abdullah Ibrahim, ibid, pp. 23-28

clapping, either. This way the song achieves an important social function which is strengthening the ties between the child and his peers and enabling him to adapt and commit to the pre-requisites of the collective game. In addition, these songs teach other educational and moral values through their simple lyrics.

Consequently, these songs:

- Provide a scientific training for the organs and senses of the child; they also provide a natural training for his motor, sensor, mental and physical powers.
- Develop the abilities and talents of the child.
- Develop the muscular, neural and mental concordance of the child.
- Raise competition and sports spirit. Songs also urge the child to succeed and excel adopting an elevated social and sports spirit.[44]

Games and Children with Special Needs

Games are considered a modern means some of dealing with some children with special needs. 'Special needs' in this context denote those people who suffer physical (motor) or mental circumstances that hinder their bodies/minds from doing complete functions.

Some people are born disabled as a result of a genetic disorder. Others are disabled due to an accident or a disease. Sometimes this disability is a natural development of an age stage: e.g. aging is a process that has several complications that need a special care. Generally, old/aging people are classified as disabled according to the degree of their health deterioration.

When talking about play as a method of dealing with disabled persons, we should state that it is an untraditional method of the alternative medicine which first appeared in the mid-twentieth century in The United States and Europe. These therapeutic methods mainly focused on using various art domains (plastic arts, theatre, music, dancing) as a co-treatment with the medical one. There are also the occupational therapy and play therapy.

---

44 Fathi AL-Šifnawi, *Madkhal Ila Dirasat Al-Maathoraat Al-Sha'beyyah Al-Ghinaeyyah (Al-Folkloor Al-Ghinaaie)* (An Introduction to Studying Popular Songs in Heritage (Folkloric Songs) SCC, 2001, p. 87

Therapeutic Play

Therapeutic play refers to a type of projection done by child during games. This treatment was first applied from the thirties to the forties in the 20th century through using dolls. Ericson made a study about gender distinctions and differences in the cubes games. Other studies focused on games that betray aggression/hostility. Therapeutic play provides the child with the environment and domains that encourage him to be spontaneous and normal in behavior. He may role-play many characters which he can never adopt in reality.

Amaster set a list of 6 means of treatment through play:

1) Play can be used in diagnosis.

2) It can be used to establish and entrench a work relationship.

3) It can be used as a break activity during the child's working day.

4) It can also be used to assist the child to deal verbally and properly with some materials and to consciously relate this to his/her feelings.

5) It can be used to develop the child's daily play procedures to whose development he may contribute in the future.

6) It can be used to help the child unconsciously to deal with materials and easily release the accompanying tension.[45]

45 Mohammad Ahmad Abdullah Ibrahim, ibid, pp. 28-31

3

HERITAGE IN POPULAR GAMES

HERITAGE IN POPULAR GAMES

The folkloric heritage or the folkloric legacy is the traditional aspect of any society's culture. We have referred to the definition of folkloric culture earlier. We must emphasize that human heritage incorporates two domains of the cognitive heritage: material/concrete and non-material/abstract. Both domains continually converge in intricate details this eventually endorses the locality of societies and their distinction.

In the following, we will give a detailed analysis of both the elements of material and non-material heritage in popular games.

First: Material Heritage in Popular Games

The environment is all the surroundings where man lives, influences others and is affected by all the creatures and objects in it. It also encompasses the human relationships among people as well as all the cultural activities made by man. With regard to this concept of environment, it becomes clear that man lives within three interlocked spheres in a continuous state of reaction. These spheres are:

<u>The Biological Sphere:</u>

It consists of water, air, metals, energy sources, plants and animals as well as the varied natural processes produced by the reactions and interactions of the environmental elements themselves e.g. photosynthesis, water cycles and the bio-cycles of other natural elements like Carbon and Nitrogen.

<u>The Social Sphere:</u>

It refers to the system and organization of human society in life, the relations among its members and the prevalent economic system.

The Cultural Sphere:

It includes whatever elements man added to environment as a result of his various activities, exploitation of natural resources and pursuit of a better life[46].

Dr Alsayed Ali asserts that there are ony two environments; the natural and cultural one.

• **First: Natural environment:** it includes all the living and non-living phenomena, organisms and other creatures surrounding man. If there are any interferences or changes in this environment, this will lead to imbalance.

• **Secondly: Cultural environment:** it is the man-made constructed environment which has two main dimensions :

• **The concrete dimension :**

It refers to all concrete innovations in housing, transportation, entertainment, clothes, agricultural methods and tools.

• **The abstract dimension:**

It includes morals, ethics, customs, traditions and thoughts. Cultural environment changes and develops according to human achievements.

The environment consists of many sub-systems that are similar to the cultural factors that influence man. These are the social, political, economical and cultural sub-systems (be they concrete and technological or abstract).

Man is affected by social factors (his relations with other individuals, and within his social and local systems), cultural factors (behaviors associated with both the concrete and abstract cultures in addition to the sum of common ethics, thoughts and concepts) as well as the political factors (factors associated with economic development)[47].

Folkloric creativity is the product of its place and environment. The interaction between man and the environment has resulted in plastic products made of materials of emotional implications to the community that created these products. There are two types of interactions between the individual and the environment: a positive and a negative one. These interactions generated traditions and emotions which man employed in singing, carving and dance arts. Eventually, these flow into the comprehensive stream of human interactions and impressions of the surrounding environment.

The environment is as influential on man as the genes. . Man is born with innate and instinctive talents; however, the environment contributes and plays its role either in developing or suppressing and eliminating them.

46 El-Sayyed 'Ali Shahdah, ibid, p. 40
47 El-Sayyed 'Ali Shahdah, ibid, p. 40

The inputs of the environment, its pre-requisites and presets provide the creator/artist with enough inspiration to fuel his innovations and creativities. Man is the product of his environment. He relies on the availability of various materials in his surroundings which, in turn, are employed as would be beneficial and fit for use by the society in this environment.

Elements of Material Heritage in Popular Games

Popular games rely on basic specific elements as follows:
1. The body as the key-player of the game.
2. Tools/toys as used in playing(be they natural or manufactured/synthetic)
3. Dolls in variant shapes
4. Plastic games that are related to art; painting, sculpture in various media/ materials, paper designs (flat or 3D) as well as synthesizing materials and formations made from the remnants of manufactured materials, and

The Art of Doll-Making as a Model of Material Heritage

Dolls are correlated to people's emotions, their life styles, skin color, as well as the materials, fabrics and costumes in the environment. They are also an embodiment of the level of the creative thinking, and the confinements and limitations on freedom that overrule these societies.

Dolls are a poor imitation of creatures. Therefore, toy-makers try as hard as possible to come up with a natural-looking, almost alive dolls which can speak, sleep and move in order to keep the audience zeal for purchase and the toy market booming.

We talk, in particular, about doll arts that reflect the surrounding environment in their shape, color, garments, jewels, ornaments, embroidery, tarots, etc. In the modern era, this art has had its audience, collectors and art galleries specialized in marketing it.

The doll displays the trails of the eras lived by societies. It could be made by children, mothers and grandmothers. It can also be made by craftsmen, artisans, educators and teachers. Dolls can be made of pottery, quilt, porcelain, paper pastes, palms' fibers (arum) or other materials of the surrounding environment.

Dolls and Folkloric Creativity

Dolls display the features of the local culture. They provide a good reading of their societies. A good artisan seeks distinction, variation, and the most genuine production and who wants to promote his craftsmanship uses his own tools and every possible means to achieve this distinction. The resources of the artisan's creativity are basically influenced by the heritage, surrounding nature and by his own needs.

Every work of art is harmoniously integrated reflecting values derived from the elements of folkloric arts such as:

1) **Material:** is the determinant of the shape and formation of dolls. It is the base of the form. It also controls the possible contour and shape of the doll. For example, wooden dolls would, by necessity, differ from those made of clay.

2) **Mass and Space:** refer to the size of the doll in its setting. Space in the formation of a doll establishes aesthetic relationships that enable better appreciation and distinction of the doll.

3) **Color:** is a basic element of the work of art and is a part of the material of the doll. It is associated with the culture, traditions and the beliefs and environmental features of the society. It also echoes people's needs and is an essential component in the doll.

4) **Motion:** adds vitality to the shape. Motion creates concordance in the work of art. The motion feature in a doll makes it more appealing and attractive because it touches the feelings, senses and imagination of the buyer/collector.

5) **Texture:** helps teach the child to discover surfaces and get acquainted with the environment. The body might be shiny or matt, smooth or rough. The art of doll-making employs texture in sculpture to emphasize the characteristics of the formation.

These arts and crafts were, and still are, one of the most unique and beloved genres that enrich the human life with its attractive shapes, forms, paintings, symbols, and distinguished colors. These features attract the attention of both the elite and the masses regardless of their classes and attitudes.

In talking about doll-making, we talk about an art that intertwines sculpture, painting, carving, textile and embroidery. It is an art that links man to the environment. Dolls are pieces of art that displays models of costumes, jewels, and head covers. Various concepts and notions engulf dolls. A doll, in its shape, is a mirror of the freedom in society, its awareness, and the depth of its plastic/artistic civilization.

The Function of Dolls

Dolls have various functions in three domains as follows:
1) The psychological function of the doll:

Artistic expression provides an outlet of emotions in an artistic shape that differs according to the material, the scope of creation and the creator, and his tools. The psychological motive of the artistic expression is providing an outlet for the person's fears and apprehensions. The importance of this outlet of motives is to achieve a balance for the artist/craftsman that leads to compatibility with the shape representing that symbol.

A person's psychological urges are the latent reasons that stimulate him to express something trough a product. A person's motives are the latent reasons that impel and enthuse him to do an action for a specific purpose. They are the real reasons behind such an action. Psychological motives are impulsive. They stir an individual's feelings towards a specific action in order to reach psychological balance.

The world of dolls provides the child with an abstract form of a living creature. Besides enabling the child to interact with the doll, his imagination is enriched, and his fear barriers against the surrounding environment are broken.

For every phase of the child's growth, there are the convenient forms of dolls through which s/he lets out many emotions talking and playing.

Every time a new feature is added to the doll, it stirs new and variant emotions for the child, hence the importance of dolls in his psychological growth.

Sound, flexibility, movability of constituent parts, harmony and the realization of the artistic values of weight, texture and size of the doll are all the criteria and inputs that influence the concepts and notions the doll introduces to the child.

The doll is the man's partner over time and place. Besides being his toy as a child, it is the present of a loving young man to his beloved. It then settles with him in his matrimonial house as an artistic piece. Moreover, it functions as a souvenir from various travels and trips. It is also a grandmother's present for her grandchild. The doll lives and accompanies man in numerous and miscellaneous moments which highlights its psychological function.

2) The social function of the doll:

The plastic/artistic product is a reflection of the society through which numerous social behaviors can be read.

The characteristics of folkloric arts are created and revealed through the interaction between the artist and the society. This interaction links the creative individuality to the public taste. It motivates the artist to express himself in the terms of his society. Therefore, the folkloric artist is the one who makes a live and vivid representation of his ideas, which are mainly his society's ideas. He is also distinguished by his vivid emotions which lead him to react. In his works, the artist seeks a psychological rhythm that depends neither on sports nor on geometry but rather on the rhythmical nature of all human actions.[48]

The society has always been the main creator of arts in accordance with its needs and the functions these arts perform. The social reality of a particular society is the space that fosters the inspiring and compelling ideas for folkloric arts. Folkloric architecture, costumes and utensils, etc. comply with a social reality and are practiced through it. If folkloric arts do not serve the society, there is no need for them.

The social dimensions affect the formation of the folkloric unit in a way that enforces and consolidates the significance and human asset of the folkloric phenomenon. Without these social dimensions, it would have no distinction and would be considered merely a handicraft production.[49]

The shapes, sizes, colors, embroideries and even the color of garments, all submit to customs of the society. In some societies, married women, widows and divorcees are to wear variant clothes to each other. Jewels and the colors of garments might even pinpoint social classification.

3) The aesthetic function of the doll:

Plastic art gives things a form. Only the form renders a work of art a production. The laws of formation embody of man's dominance over substance. They are also the means of preserving human experience and transferring it to future generations. They are a necessity for art and life. Importantly enough, form in artistic products is linked to a function.

Art is closely-related to skills. Not only because all visual and plastic arts depend on learning how to use one tool or another, but because these arts also rely on the ability to form things up to the will and whims of the artist.

48 Mahmoud Elshaal, *Adaah Asaaseyyah Lilkashf 'An Al-Haqaeq Al-Kawneyyah Wa Al-Qeyam Al-Gamaleyyah Magallat Al-Finoun Al-Sha'beyyah* (A Basic Tool for Recognizing Universal Facts and Aesthetic Values). Magllat Al-Finoun Al-Sha'beyyah (Folkloric Arts Magazine).Vol. 24, GEBO, Cairo, 1989

49 Arnest Fisher, The Necessity of art. Trans. As'ad Haleem. GEBO, Cairo, 1998

50 Herbert Reed, *Art Today*. Translator: Mohammad Fathi Hassan & Gerges 'Abdo, Cairo, GEBO, 1981

However, art is more than just skills. A skill is a functional job associated with crafts. Art starts wherever functions end. Art refines a job with no interference with it.[51]

The practical or aesthetic function (or both of them) is the target of the folkloric plastic product. Man needs housing, clothes, food and beverage in order to live. He resorts to the folkloric artist to innovate everything that would help him to live. Eventually, the artist comes out with a creation/product that performs a particular task in the daily life.

The aesthetic dimension is related to the color, texture, and value the same degree as it is related to shape, mass and space which are all basic elements of the formation.

The Shapes of Dolls

Dolls have taken the shapes of various creatures that have been granted a tint of mystery and power because of their being represented in myths. For example:

*Human figures: e. g. man (in the shape of a knight, a servant, a king or a clown) or a woman (in the shape of a bride, a grandmother or a dancer) Each of these characters would be typically represented in accordance to his/her social role and class.

*Animal: e.g. farm animals or pets such as: a camel, a horse, a donkey, a monkey, a bear, a dog, a cat, a lion, a rabbit, a lamb, a sheep, etc.

*Birds: e.g. a hoopoe, a peacock, a sparrow, a pigeon, a dove, a cock, a chick, a duck, etc.

*Reptiles: e.g. a chameleon, a lizard, a turtle, a snake, etc.

*Amphibians: e.g.an alligator, a hippopotamus, fishes, sea turtles, etc.

*Insects: e.g. a scorpion, a scarab, etc.

*Plants: e.g. botanic ornaments filling the blanks in the sculpture of the doll's body.

*Professionals figures: e.g. a huntsman, a carpenter, a soldier, a farmer, a thief, etc.

*Vehicles: e.g. a plane, a car, a boat or a bicycle.

*Architectural forms: e.g. squares and balconies.

51 Mahmoud Al-Basuiony, *Toroq Ta'allom Al-Finoun* (Methods of Learning Art), Dar Al-Ma'aref, Cairo, 1994

Materials

The materials used in doll-making are miscellaneous. Dolls could be made of various materials such as fur, plastic, paper, clay, cotton, gauze, wool, arum, porcelain, etc.

Dolls and Folkloric Costumes

Folkloric costumes hold a place in legends and myths. They give us a clear picture of some of the traditions and beliefs associated with our costumes in past times. They are not intended merely for clothing, they also have another function associated with and enriching traditional imagination. It is a spiritual function correlated to the subconscious feelings. In ancient civilizations, people's history and also their future hopes were inscribed and embroidered on their clothing…The traditional man wraps himself in his myths and illusions which sometimes encapsulate rare values that, in spite of the depth of their meanings and their genuineness, are discarded because of their repulsive appearances[52].

Handmade Versus Manufactured Dolls

In the Arab world, handmade dolls are associated with the poor community. Currently, handmade dolls suffer from poor marketing and low demand. As a result of the rare and decreasing desire to deal with the traditional handmade products, craftsmen give up working in traditional crafts. The purchase of manufactured dolls made of plastics or fabrics has prevailed.

Earlier, parents not only participated in making dolls for children, they played with them as well. Because of it is being used mainly by the poor and the marginalized, currently, the application of handicraft to the product is confined to a small number of craftsmen. This resulted in a low level product made of poor quality material as would fit its being sold cheaper. This is the case with most handicrafts which did not succeed in being modified and blooming into a handmade tourist-oriented product. As for other localized products, they became the commodity of the poor class which prefers them because of their cheap prices and the availability of their materials.

52 Saad Al-khadem, *Al-Fan Al-Sha'abi Wa Al-Mo'ataqadat Al-Sehreyyah* (Folkloric Art and Magical Beliefs). Maktabat Al-NahĎah, Cairo, N.D

Durability Features in Dolls

Dolls have several characteristics that ensure their durability through time and place. These are:
1) Flexibility.
2) Changeability.
3) Development according to the changing nature of societies.
4) Appealing to the symbolic nature of the child.
4) Adaptability to the traditions and circumstances of the place.
5) Adaptability to development through time.
6) Adaptability to technological evolution.
7) Modifiability to fit families of various levels.

Second: Verbal Heritage in Popular Games

Definition of the Verbal/Non-concrete Heritage:
Verbal heritage denotes all the legacy related to sayings and paroles. It is associated with the beliefs, customs and knowledge passed on from one generation to another in an attempt to preserve and bequeath them as part of the local features and particularity of a culture. Following, we will focus on the verbal heritage associated with games.

Songs as a Model of the Verbal Heritage Correlated to Game Performances

Children correlate specific songs to games. These functional songs are correlated to the movements of the body performing the game. They help the child control his body movements and perform them harmoniously with his limbs. They are also associated with the playing stage of the children.

It is rare to find a song performed by children without accompanying body movements as would be necessary in the game or the mini-play. These movements are designed to that match the awareness of the children and their simple experiences. Accordingly, these songs employ mostly a limited range of melodies and require simple voice potentialities. They employ very few music transitions that would fit the untrained voices and the simple potentialities and music capabilities of the children. Their rhythmical and melodic sequences also agree with the tempo of the game or motion of the mini-dramatic performance. So, the inner rhythm of the song sets the tempo of the motion as determined by the meter of the lyrics, the scansion of regular and simple foot as well as the rhyme. These songs maintain the cadence of the lyrics regardless of its meaning or even the linguistic coherence of its words and ideas. The lyrics are more likely to be trivial words of rather irrational meanings. Several examples of this type of songs bear similar meanings and have the same general targets. These are found in the majority of the heritage of children's songs and games around the Arab world.[53]

Children's songs are categorized into many forms; some of which are correlated to popular games. These are subdivided as follows:

1) Songs with fixed lyrics and melody that can accompany any game without being associated with a specific one. Their importance lies in the value of their cadence and rhythm.

2) Songs which accompany and are inseparable of specific games. These games set and follow the motion of the game and the plot of the dramatic action of the play. In these songs, children cast roles and characters and every child performs a specific role.[54]

3) Songs used during the preparation for the game, choice of players, and casting the roles of its players. These do not accompany the game itself.[55]

The Song and Game of the Noohi (Pitch-Black) Raven as a Model

In this game a group of girls (sometimes young boys are allowed as well) play the role of birds, standing in a line behind one of them (the elder and the bigger). Every player holds the girl before her by the waist and in front of them stands a boy or a girl playing the role of the raven who tries to snatch one of them. The mother defends her girls and behind her the group dodges and maneuvers in an attempt to escape from the raven.

The game is accompanied by recursive singing by the three parties: the raven, the mother and the birds. These lines are dramatically and rhythmically sung without the accompaniment of any musical instruments or clapping, etc. as follows:[56]

> The raven: I'm the noohi noohi raven. I snatch and fly on the roof,
> on the roof.
> The mother: You would not dare, (sarcastically) O' ye the apple of

53 Fathi AL-Šifnawi, ibid, p. 87
54 Fathi AL-Šifnawi, ibid, p. 87
55 Ibid, pp. 97-98
56 Ibid, p. 91

my eye. I'm their mum and I will protect them. If I live, I would
bring them up well. If I die, they'd break their necks.

The raven: I dropped a bunch of money. (cadenced performance).

The group: Liar, liar. Liar, liar.

The raven: I swear to God I lost it.

The group: Liar, liar. Liar, liar.

The raven: Give me your dearest one.

The mother: No, I won't.

The raven: Give me your dearest one.

The mother: Who would cook for me?

The raven: I would cook for you.

The mother: Who would knead for me?

The raven: I would knead for you.

After such debate, the raven, all of a sudden, attacks to snatch one of the
girls and tug her (if he succeeded) behind him in a row. The game goes on
until the mother's line is finished and she is left all alone. Thence, she herself
becomes the raven, and the children restart the game.

Mohamed Hasan Ghanem, in his book Children's Singing, says, "songs
develop skills which I consider the same as those provided by games for the
child." These skills are:[57]

1) Mental skills: such as decision-making, problem-solving, sound
planning, continuous self-learning, mature thinking, research and scrutiny,
creativity and innovation, as well as predicting events.

2) Social skills: e. g. shouldering responsibility, cooperation, participation,
decent competition, establishing balanced relationships with others. The
last entails give and take relations, accepting differences in opinion or in
characteristics, self and others' respect, the ability to negotiate, the ability to
lead, the ability to give refusals politely and to express one's feelings decently
without hurting others' feelings).

3) Emotional skills: such as the ability to control feelings, to forgive, to
handle pressures, to be flexible and tolerant, to appreciate others' feelings, to
face them, as well as self-restraint, willpower, good-heartedness.

57 Mohammad Hassan Ghanim, ibid, pp. 123-124

The Function of Verbosity in Game Performance

A song in a game may have one/all of these functions:

- Organizing the movement between players.
- Balancing the distribution of movements of the limbs of the performer's body.
- Giving psychological motivating to the competitors.
- Securing the enjoyment of the dynamic and motor performance within the group.
- Stirring positive feelings and emotions during the game.

Festivals and Popular Games

Several games are associated to public festivals. For example the following events have relevant popular games:

1. Religious Ceremonies:

For example, the festivalities held in the month of Ramadan where children gather to decorate streets and spend time in playing games and songs all over popular districts.

2. National Ceremonies:

Some games are related to national occasions. This affected some game products e.g. the toys and lanterns featuring Hassan Nasrallah and Saddam Hussein. With the application of technology in game/toy manufacturing the use of such symbols became widespread and applicable. Hence, a new interactional medium has been established between games and political events.

3. Nature:

There are games associated with and dependent on natural features such as the internal assortments on beaches. These natural phenomena are the actual beginnings of a child's sense of architecture, place, space, mass and relativity. There is also the phenomenon of 'full moon' which is associated with numerous games and songs which are widespread in the Egyptian Delta and all over Egypt.

4. Social Occasions:

Some games are related to social occasions especially birth and marriage. Songs are a main feature in all aspects of social life.

4

GAMES AND THE UNIVERSAL IDENTITY

GAMES AND THE UNIVERSAL IDENTITY

The world has one origin. However varied are the shapes and appearances it incorporates, these ultimately form an integrated whole. Games are one of performative arts which highly reflect and emphasize this concept. Games are a main part of human heritage. They play a big role in child upbringing and also in man's life at all ages: the young, youths and the elderly as well. They are a rich genre of legacy inputs which inspire many people with miscellaneous concepts and symbolic connotations. Games bear rich forms and details of the elements of the traditional heritage passed on from a generation to another.

Playing is an established social and communicative method. A child can acquire social communication, understand his elders' roles and try to imitate them through playing. Through playing with his peers, he learns the acceptable social values, understands social networking, gives up his selfishness and adapts to the environment.

Therefore, it is important to use playing in accordance with our need for an effective universal unity. Working on the principles of the unity and integration of the universe is a current necessity in all our relations especially when communication between the different worlds and the divergent interests of states are very poor. If we re-established human cooperation upon the principles of partnership and integration, this would certainly positively affect growth on this planet.

If we look at the traditional games from a developmental perspective with a social, political, and economic enactment, we may unify the thresholds of human pleasure and happiness with our partners.

Identity

The concept of identity has been related to human groupings ever since the very beginning of universe. Idiosyncrasy in every group began to have its features through the body characteristics and symbols which distinguished it.

When René Descartes says "I think; therefore I am", identity comes before subjectivity and idiosyncrasy.

Identity has always been the codified data set by the West in the modern world. The goal is to designate and typify every one's information into data about place of birth, country, residence, etc.

Identity cards, personal papers and documents are just 'the identity' to designate man as being….'himself'. These documents which are superficially used to check and verify a person's identity are simply a systematized means of racialism.

In Arabic,the word *huweyyah* 'identity' is derived from the word *huwwah* denoting the essence and truth of an object. Identity also denotes 'uniqueness' and singularity. Cultural identity denotes cultural uniqueness involving all aspects of culture such as traditions, behaviors, norms, morals, values, and life perspective.[58]

Identity is an old legacy word explained in terminology references such as Algergany's **Al-Ta'arifaat** (Definitions). In this book and also in Western dictionaries *identity* means that "a thing be itself, having no counterpart or equivalent." In his **Al-Hrouf**, Al-Faraaby defined 'identity' as the opposite of the concept of 'othernesses. Otherness might be relative rather than exclusive; in this case the opposition between identity and otherness becomes common. In Arabic legacy, variation is more common identicality. Linguistically speaking, *ikhtilaaf* 'variation' is a simple derivative word/noun whereas *huweyyah* is a compound noun of a discrete pronoun *huwa* 'he' which has no derivative or synonyms.

Identity is originally a philosophical topic. It was tackled by the Existentialists and Idealists. They made it a law, known as Identity

58 Mohammad Almunir, *Al'awlamah Wa 'Aalam Bila Huweyyah* (Globalization and A World without Identity). 2000

59 Hassan Hefni, *Al-Huweyyah* (Identity), Cairo, SCC, 2012, p. 17

Law. For some philosophers, like Nietzsche, it is the primal law in thought and in Existentialism. The concept of otherness is not a variant discrete law, rather it is just an exclusion of the identity/ego. This leaves us with the controversial issue of the 'supreme ego'.[60]

A community's identity is not eternally constant or of an internal origin. The development of an identity is subject to external influences and the international circulation of ideas, cultures and civilizations. It is also related to the power conflicts in every society. Such conflicts are instigated either directly or indirectly by the external influences, the balances/imbalance of large geo-political areas and the competitions among the regional and international countries.[61]

The effacement of an identity is the elimination of the distinctive features of the culture which distinguish it against variant cultures. Identity establishes the concepts which endow every culture its unique values and idiosyncrasies. It is the national character whose absence thaws the main and distinctive features among nations. Identity sows a sense which makes of its existence as a collective feeling a prop and support for the peculiar heritage of its community.

Identity is also associated with the distinctive features of an object upon which its idiosyncrasy, distinction and uniqueness are based. It is the totality of the mutual relations between an object and the other objects interactive with it and the depth of their interrelationship.

The writer thinks that identity is a mirror and reflection of affiliations. Accordingly, an identity can be classified as follows:[62]

Religious identity: it is the affiliation to a specific religion, sect or belief. This affects clothes, food, appearance and content in different ways proportionally to the influence of and commitment to the the religious identity and reference.

60 Hassan Hefni, Nischte; *The Resistance Philosopher.* Egyptain Philosophic Society, Cairo, 2003, pp.181-192

61 Khalaf Bisheer, *Al-Huweyyah Wa Al-ʿAwlamah* (Identity and Globalization), Al-Shrouk Newspaper, Algeria, 2006. Quoted by Dr.Mohammad ʿAbed Al-Gaabry, a speech in the forum "Al-Touraath Wa Taḥadeyyat Al-ʿAsr" (Heritage and Challenges of the Age)

62 Eman Mahran, *Tanmeyyat Al_heraf Al-Taqleedeyyah Madkhlan lilhifaaz ʿAla Al-huweyyah* (Developing Traditional Crafts: An Approach To Preserve Identity). SCC, Cairo, 2009.

Social identity: it is the affiliation to a community or a clan with its traditions, concepts and acceptable /unacceptable values. In this case the person follows a group.

National identity: it is the affiliation to the culture of a specific country, region or homeland and the different orientations dictated by its history and national features.

Economic identity: it is the affiliation to an economic system whether by an individual or a community.

Locative identity: it is the affiliation created because of the unity of places in their distinctive geographical and demographic features. In this case identity correlates to the locative factors and their geographical indications.

Most of the traditional games, old sports and performative forms of expression which reflect the cultures of aboriginal peoples and the inherited daily lifestyles embody the common identity of humanity. Many minute details of these games were already wiped away. Those which are still alive are prone to erosion and disappearance due to the influence of the common factors and the adaptation between globalization and the rich and variant sports legacy. Eventually, traditional and sport games become an asset through cultural understanding and mutual tolerance between communities and states. This, in turn, contributes to the enlightenment about peace culture.

The Pillars of Identity

Language, belief and geography are among the most critical factors of the integrating or disintegrating of the identity which distinguish an area from another. They affect the individual in all fields of life. If linguistic unity is dismantled, affiliation may disintegrate and a common dialogue will not be possible. In case of the differences in religious identity, which outlines social life and defines taboos, the forbidden and the allowed, all these domains will certainly, by necessity, be variant. Moreover, boundaries and delimitations within the same place would initiate differences which may depart from the concept of common identity.[63]

When people share the same history and geography, they will surely have one and the same identity. Identity is a mutual bond between groups. It embodies the heritage which gathers people around a meeting point; be it a language, a belief or a lifestyle.

63 Eman Mahran, ibid, 2009

This meeting point, which is a collective emotion, is reflection of a common history, geography and influences. All these factors create harmony and rapprochement in several general features of that group so that it would have a representative identity of homogeneous concordant elements.

Identity is the national personality without which a nation falls. It is the national character whose absence vanishes the nation's main features. We here talk about identity as a mirror of interaction over generations in the crafts history and in the art heritage of states. Inherited arts, including public games, involve numerous details which can be used to serve and entrench the organic unity of society.

The Universal Identity

The universal identity is based on the common among human beings regardless of any differences in belief, culture, gender, colour or homeland. We are all human beings who have a body, feelings and share the same basic needs.

The universal identity respects idiosyncrasy and benefits from it. It also respects the nature of communities. It endorses the universal dimension in the man as a creature in this universe. The universal identity relies on the common factors. For example, we are all human beings with feelings and a body where the same red blood moves. The delimitations of our mental and cognitive abilities are set by our being a different species. The universal identity contributes to reinforcing culture's principles, respect for the other's culture and communication and integration between communities and cultures. This, in turn, creates and establishes dialogue among peoples and decreases points for negative friction among cultures.

The universal identity is the opposite of globalization. The first term respects privacy and benefits from idiosyncrasy. The later, on the other hand, wipes away privacy for many interests, on top of which the economic ones. Globalization harms the economy and culture of the poor countries for the sake of the rich ones.

The universal identity respects the nature of people and their sacred objects. It highlights the universal dimension in man as being a creature in this universal system regardless of any minor differences.

It also respects variety in experience. It is an identity that incorporates the miscellaneous and variant as its constituents. It is associated with the human unity and is an introduction to the human brotherhood.

The writer thinks that several concepts are relevant to the universal identity as follows:

• The political concept of the universal identity:

The universal identity is firmly related to the political will which governs the world. This political will lies in the hands of a group of countries which control institutions, international decisions, economy and mass media. Consequently, the universal identity will be shaped to the vision of these countries which have the political will and will also lie under their control. Accordingly, other countries in the world will be dominated by the interests of these hegemonizing countries. This drives us apart from the will of several people who aspire for social peace and also far from the poor world which does not own its political decision. If so, many problems will surface in these rich countries which are in a need of social peace and security in the universe to live with others on earth. These hegemonizing countries would, then, need to re-establish their vision within the framework of the universal identity in order to achieve universal peace.

• The economic concept of the universal identity:

With the over-rule of a globalization law of an economic origin, a gap between the powerfully economic and productive world and the poor world was created. This poor world owns nothing but the materials with no machinery or economic tools. Its markets are open for and flooded with the products of the developed countries. Therefore, the economic concept of the universal identity needs fair laws which provide man and his brother with equal legal rights so that he can live and exist as well.

Some organizations like the Fair Trade Federation set solutions to this problem. For example, this federation sponsors traditional and hand-made products and renders them tax-free on materials, exportation and exhibitions because they are produced in poor countries in the world.

• The social concept of the universal identity:

Human knowledge shares the same principles and social values that have been agreed upon ever since human life and social relations were established and organized. Communities share the values of love of life, peaceful communication and a desire for stability and security.

It is the human identity which makes the scene of killing a child like the Palestinian Mohammed Aldurrah(a young boy killed in his father's hands) stir the same painful feelings in any person regardless of his nationality, religion or identity. The proximity of social life systems in many areas of the world and the similarity in the form of families and communities urges us to believe in the social unity of the universe.

• **The cultural concept of the universal identity:**

Culture is related to the tidal movements of development. Human communication overseas, through journeys and trade over the history depended on interrelatedness and partnership.

In the modern age, Complications and political boundaries hindered the direct commercial communication among people in favor of the interests of political and economic governments.

Modern politics enforced control over territories, boundaries and international supreme decisions. This lead to the appearance of a political classification of countries which harms culture and the industrially developing countries. The super-fast transportations and hegemony of the international mass media promoting the interests of some countries over those of others resulted in the elimination and extinction of specific percepts. This sow hatred among cultures and severed communicational links in many areas.

All these factors work against the concept of our common universal identity. They promote a specific culture over other ones so that we live in an international cultural driftage of specific identities.

With a cultural viewpoint of the universal identity, communities may be allowed their legal rights. Eventually integration, co-existence and communication will be achieved between different cultures in our cultural context and universe.

The Universal Identity and the Clash of Civilizations

Samuel Huntington, in his book **The Civilization's Clash**, says, "Conflict between civilizations will dominate the international political affairs. The differences and distinctions between civilizations will be the war line in the future. If there is a future world war, it will be a war of civilizations".

On the other hand, some thinkers endorse the idea of dialogue between civilizations. For example, John Espozeto, the famous American researcher, defends this point of view on basis that understanding 'the other' and 'tolerance' with his differences and strangeness could establish a dialogue and mutual dependence that would prevent such violent actions. The main idea in Espozeto's book Islamic Threat a Reality or Fable? is that Islam for the west represents a challenge rather than a threat. As for the Arabs,they use the term 'tolerance' in their literature with other lexical items in their discourse which is characterized by weakness and inability.[64]

There are great similarities in songs and games of children they play and perform all over the world. They have the same features and uniforms characteristics in composition, melodic structure and tonal sequence.

They are also similar in their motor nature depending on both the outer shape of a child and his/her bodily, muscular, motor, psychological and vocal buildup. These elementary songs and games match his primal and simple abilities. The song would be very simple, short and easy to the extent that it can be oratory rather than melodic which fits the child's motor, mental and artistic abilities and his/her need for playing and activity.

Songs and games are considered the most prominent and typical activities in of human childhood. The child deeply indulges into them with a pure innocence that embodies this important, fresh and carefree life stage. Games and play for the child at that age are not timed or scheduled. S/he can play whenever s/he wants with whoever s/he wants and whichever way they like. There are tens of songs related to games which have surely been known from old ages. These songs were composed by the children themselves or their mothers and the elderly. More than three thousand years ago, in the tombs of Ḥotb, who was a member of the fifth old Egyptian dynasty, there is graffiti which portray several types of popular games some which are still known and performed in Egypt.[65]

Following is an example for these game-related songs is the Lebanon. The song says:

O' haji Mohammad…yo yo…!!!	Ya Ḥagag Mohammad. . yoyo. .
How sooty you are!!! yo yo!!!	Qaddeish miŠmmad. . yoyo
Sooty like Masryyeh…yo yo!!!	MiŠmmad maŠryyah. . yoyo.
As would fill a temneyyah (kitchen cupboard)…yo yo!!!	Malwe el-tamneyya. . yoyo
Whose temneyyah??…. yo yo!!!	Tamnyyet meen. . yoyo
*********	**********
My uncle Shaheen …yo yo!!!	'Amy Shaheen. . yoyo…..

64 Qasim 'Abdouh Qasim, Al-Muslimoon Wa Ouroppa ;Al-TaTawor Al-Tareekhi LiŠourat Al-Aakhar (Muslims and Europe; Development of the ther's Image over History). GEBO. 2012. p. 187

65 Fathi AL-Šifnawi, Madkhal Ila Dirasat Al-Maathoraat Al-Sha'beyyah Al-Ghinaeyyah (Al-Folkloor Al-Ghinaaie) (An Introduction to Studying Popular Songs in Heritage (Folkloric Songs) SCC, 2001, p. 63

Shaheen did not die…yo yo!!!

Shaheen ma maat. . yoyo…

He has daughters…yo yo!!

'Ando banaat. . yoyo….. .

They are so black…. yo yo!!!

Banaato. . sood. . yoyo…

****

****

O'for the unfortunate. . yo yo!!!

Bakht el-maw'ood. . yoyo…

He begot Fattoom (endearment name of a girl called Fatimah)…yo yo!!!

Khallaf FaTToom. . yoyo..

She eats and moos…yo yo!!

Takol we tzoom. . yoyo…

And his nine daughters. . yo yo!!

We banaato tes'aah. . yoyo…

Crouching and eating from the tray…yo yo!!

A'adeen 'ala el-aŠ'ah. . yoyo[66]

Dolls and Wars of Identity

Dolls are the product of their cultures. They embody a part of people's thought and attitude in their communities. *Barby* the American blond doll was promoted in the markets as a model for the girls to look up to and follow. It succeeded to be the dream of young girls to have. It over crossed its territory and has become a world model that set *Barby* as a booming cultural and commercial project. This project pillared the American girl as a model of beauty and attractiveness among young girls in this world. I see this as a part of the American policy to overrule the world through food, songs and cinema. It is an essential component of the policy of the overspreading Anglo-American policy to impose the western modern model of modernity on the world market.

The black doll *Sara-Li*, which appeared in the mid-sixties in the twentieth century, represented the period of racial discrimination in American history period. This doll embodied extreme racialism in the American community.

Both the doll *Razan*, embodying the Muslim girl staying in the west, and the veiled eastern doll Fulla, the eastern veiled doll, appeared at the early nineties of the twentieth century. Two other Iranian dolls Dara and Sara, appeared in the same period expressing and joining the war between cultures for the protection of Islamic national identity in the Arab world with its localities.

---

66 Fathi AL-Šifnawi, ibid.

Here, we can see the conflict between cultures that poses the question: which identity is more dominant in the Islamic world the national or the religious?

Dolls and the Issue of Affiliation

Dolls are an important part of local culture. A doll, very simply and briefly, embodies an essential part of the privacy and idiosyncrasy of a culture whose existence denotes a package of morals and concepts epitomizing many stages of the reinforcement of affiliation.

Toys play a role in endorsing and promoting national identity in the countries of the world. They also closely reflect the viewpoint of the crafts artist about his community's history.

Toys can affect affiliations particularly those of young children. They very simply ingrain in them belief and confidence in their heritage for they are embodiments of history.

Therefore, this thought and orientation which is based on the reality and locality of the geographical region should be adopted.

Popular Games and the Acceptance of the Other's Culture

Popular games are not ascribed to a specific ethnic or religious identity. They incorporate symbols as elements of the games. A game may even include symbols of various cultures. Games are open to other cultures. This has been the method through which the common and varied elements between cultures which are intertwined in the verbal and motor performance of playing and games. The phrase 'the other's culture' here denotes variant cultures whose elements are not completely in accordance with the individual's mother culture.

In popular games players keep adding up elements till they eventually come up with a variant game product. This is, of course, a means and a proof of a true communication and acceptance of the other. Moreover, it enriches human culture with new and varied versions of the game.

Games are a mirror of achieving justice as would appear in the process of casting roles regardless of any complicated classifications. Games rather depend on a classification of the real potentialities for playing…Games are different because they are a mirror of nature unlike human beings who self-consciously set hierarchical classifications as imposed by historical layers.

Games are life in its simple and just form without the classifications which tainted man all through history. Popular games realize the concept of social justice in its simplest form.

Playing is a Universal Language
We all Play, We are all Human

Games are considered a universal language employing the same miscellaneous dimensions such as physical expression and vocal performance. We will elaborate on an example shown in the preamble of Misses Baheegah Rasheed's book[67] where she discusses similarity between popular games in the world, as follows:

The Songs of Popular Games in Human Culture

If we thoroughly examine popular songs and games in numerous countries, we will discover several similarities. Some of these games are almost a carbon copy of their counterparts in other countries.

For example various forms of ball games, hopscotch, jump rope, hopping and leaping games, running and competitions are all common games among all children in the world.

The games *El-ta'lab fat fat* (The fox ran and ran) and *Ya meheela helli helli* (O'beuaty, untie, untie….) have their French counterparts in the two games *Ainis Font Les Petites Marionettes* and *Le Renard Passé, Passé.*

There are many other examples of similar games. This ultimately invites us to raise the question about the origin of these games and songs which are similar in form and content despite the remote distances between their countries and the different environments, languages, customs, traditions and moral values? Other questions are: Which was/were their mother environment(s)? How did they develop? How were they transferred from one environment to another? And so on.

If we regard these games and songs as a genre which is close to primitive and elementary forms of music, we will find answers to all these questions in the book by the knowledgeable German writer Kortz Zaks The Rise of Music in The Ancient World East and West.

Baheegah ended her words at this point, but we would like to reflect on

---

67 Baheegah Rasheed, ibid.

the futuristic vision encapsulated in her words. This futuristic vision calls for a comprehensive scientific forum which gathers both western and eastern scientists to discuss the concept of game songs based on her perspective. The growth and upbringing of children is proportional to the growth of their communities through history and the accumulation of human experiences between the East and West. Songs, accordingly, provide a reading of the human communication in the world of game songs.

5

GAMES AND DIGITAL TECHNOLOGY

GAMES AND DIGITAL TECHNOLOGY

Technology in the modern world contributed to the spread of specific games and the popularity of others. Multimedia also contributed to the booming appeal of thousand electronic games all over the world.

Technology, here, refers to the modern technical progress which devised many innovative solutions. These solutions contributed to the speedy growth of the technological sciences and guaranteed technological products fast promotion, cheaper prices and worldwide popularity. Digital technology has both advantages and disadvantages as will be displayed below.

The Advantages of the Digital Technology:

Digital technology facilitates using modern appliances. It secures rapid promotion of products everywhere and at all levels. It also guarantees the cheapness, variety of forms, tastes and levels in response to the varied needs of different markets in this world. Digital technology appeals to the eye. Its spare parts and maintenance are available. Its speedy and successive upgrades made it multifunctional and open for several possibilities and users. Moreover, appliances of digital technology save a lot of time in doing complicated and sophisticated jobs.

The Disadvantages of the Digital Technology:

The main disadvantage of digital technology is that it encourages individualism over communicativeness with the society. It almost isolates the individual in a virtual world with no communications with others. This reduces the interactive experiences between a person and his surrounding environment and confines his social abilities which would enrich him with valuable experiences.

The Technological Employment of Electronic Games

Multimedia has spread through several means particularly personal mobile phones. Various games have been and could be uploaded on these phones which are available to a wide range of consumers. It became easy and cheap to play these games. As a result they have become available to every age and social class. Accordingly, we can state that technology has been employed to serve and promote these dynamic and interactive games.

Dolls and Electronic Games

Cartoons and computer games opened a wide market for manufactured mass-production dolls. The technological revolution man is living in modern age made the computer fundamental for families.

Progress made mobile phones have the same potentialities of the computer. Various games and artistic materials can be easily downloaded/uploaded on it, which is a significant shift in children and adults games as well. However, handicraft dolls maintain their charm and association with the traditional mother culture because electronic games appeal only to a specific range of consumers.

There is the experience of Disney Land in creating cartoons and 3D films and investing these imaginary characters in manufacturing dolls. This experience was later followed by launching Barbie, the doll, which has become a heroine of a series of cartoons of successful marketing and promotion of the American cultural models. Both these American models deserve study and analysis.

Games and Promoting Cultures

Polarization is the implicit attraction of the consumer. It relies on arousing sympathy and attracting the public whenever culture is closer to the feelings. Games hold the key to dealing with people. They rely on an implicit attraction because they are close to culture.

The idea of promoting various cultures is based on merchandising culture and cultural products through new, technological and digital games. As a result of being open to incorporate materials and symbols that promote a particular culture, these games are being more marketed than appliances. They could easily promote specific ideas as well as cultural products. They became more of a tool, a method, and a channel than a target.

Games and Modern Cultural Wars

The modern cultural war is the war where new visions and practices are consolidated and entrenched against the traditional and the local idiosyncrasies of societies.

Cultural replacement is the most dangerous future war. Fashion, innovations and the new and exotic along with commercial bedazzlement, all might include several terms, phrases, and stories along with their characters that gradually lead to the cultural replacement of certain notions. These displaced notions might not relate to the local minds of different regions nor respect the concept of the cultural idiosyncrasies of every society.

Social idiosyncrasy is the safety valve of societies. It denotes the variant which every society cherishes and preserves. It is the societal distinction that could be ancient heritage or a modern tradition of specific connotations accepted by the community. Hence, it is necessary to preserve the essential features of this idiosyncrasy that distinguishes the society.

The Conflicts of Cultural Idiosyncrasies

The word 'conflict' here is not used in the traditional political sense. It rather denotes placing and supporting cultural idiosyncrasy against its counter target which displaces it so that it appear dull within the light of updated inputs. Thus, in time, this different and variant would fade away and lose many of its opposing and distinguishing features.

The war of cultural identities and idiosyncrasies is the future Third World War. It is an unrevealed one that is launched in every incoming product or culture which complies with the commercial laws of globalization. These commercial laws ensure the dissolution of the distinctive cultural elements replacing the concept of 'that which is peculiar to' with 'all is generalized' is the basic target of this war.

Modern games with their notions which counter the authenticity and originality of local societies are a medium of declaring war against locality and idiosyncratic symbols.

The idea of the generalization of connotations, re-structuring and re-allocation is highly complicated. Modern technological devices, and the games and movies uploaded on multimedia, as well as the simplicity of dealing with the symbols, relationships, and game techniques facilitate the over-domination of a specific collective mind as would be desired and funded by particular money. For example, drug money could be used to promote concepts or products which are explicitly and openly discarded by society. Other examples are:

- Explicitly highlighting and promoting the denounced primitive regressive thought through the polarization of the binary concepts of good and bad, victory and defeat, and submission as preached through dramatic performance helps entrench the ideologies of radical religious groups of heavenly or non-heavenly religions.

- Explicitly or implicitly highlighting and promoting drug addiction, using weapons, etc. is rejected and denounced. However,modern technology and multimedia employment are associated with the violent state these abusive materials create. They are consumer-oriented, especially to adolescents who like to discover and explore and are easily stirred and directed.

Electronic Games and Ideological Wars

In the modern world, we undergo strange conflicts that never existed in the previous ages of the human history. We live in a world ruled by racist concepts as well as other underlying meanings. A world which -ruled over by commercial laws of globalization-does not acknowledge cultural pluralism.

For example, in electronic games, you will find scenes of real fighting that necessitate extreme observation and concentration. While virtually fighting in the game, you may become a target and in return you have a target to hit. The exchange of fight here depends on the strongest and cleverest in chasing, pursuit and observation. Thus the key-concept chosen and endorsed by the designers of electronic games of which there are thousands is conflict and war.

These electronic games accredit the mental skill of observation and speedy reaction. However, the promotion of the concepts of conflict and competition, and the exaltation in negative abhorred actions (e.g. violence and killing) belittle this single advantage. Eventually, they increase the hostility and aggressiveness of the child/player as well as his competitive sense.

Several aspects in life need flexibility and tolerance on part of the individual to be able to deal with them on a daily basis. With the increasing time and devotion of players to electronic war games, they start developing new qualities such as individualism rather than team spirit and negativity rather than positiveness. Therefore, electronic war games are considered a destructive tool of the life of the modern highly-pressurized man.

Promoting Electronic Games for Children in the Developing World

Weaponry is as old in the world as humanity. Its markets depend on and cater for conflict regions in the world. Weaponry is continually fed with new users. Weaponry market is the most blossoming market in the world. At a time when political solutions are superficial, slow and stumbling, weaponry becomes the realistic effective alternative.

THE END: The minds and thoughts of young children and teenagers are now over dominated by electronic war games concurrently with millions of plastic toy pistols and weaponry machines flooding African and Arab markets.

CONCLUSION

Games are a collective creativity related to the cultural surroundings. Playing is a means of modeling nature and the ever- moving and going globe. Games are an authentic component in the human culture. They have never been confined to one gender, race, social level or age. Accordingly, to safeguard this human phenomenon is to maintain an important element of folkloric legacy. Popular games bear a cultural component as portrayed -for example- in the popular and popular games portrayed on walls of pharaonic temples.

Games display a large variety of symbols and physical performances associated with the environment. Games are also susceptible to changes in time, place and social and economic variables.

In addition to miscellaneous performances games have also, psychological and educational aspects and a social role that endorse the player harmony and concordance with his surroundings.

Games are considered both a material and abstract legacy. On the one hand, they are associated with the local materials of the environment .On the other, they are associated with man, the tools, toys and puppets created with the crafty hands. These unique toys and tools are so artistically, psychologically and socially laden that they incorporate much of traditional culture of society.

Technology has a great influence on the popularity, variation and change of both the functions and concepts of games. Although games in the age of globalization are commercially-bound, emphasizing their universal identity could participate in promoting more positive values and concepts about human communication and about games as well.

RECOMMENDATIONS

Following are recommendations to emphasize the role of popular games from a perspective of human partnership and universal identity:

1.Holding workshops about popular games and their role in communicating values in order to promote human rights and equality between all parties in society.

2.Holding local and international festivals all over the world in order to highlight the cultural variations of human race.

3. Developing traditional collective/group games in local society would spread community peacefulness and encourage interaction between various social levels.

4.Holding international academic workshops among specialists in order to set a common strategy regarding popular games.

5.Reviving folkloric legacy through the technological investment of its local items.

6.Cooperating with research institutions and authorities in order to effectuate the futuristic views of researchers bout popular games.

7.Building multilingual websites in various domains to spread knowledge about popular games.

8.Providing financial for publishing researches, books and publications about human legacy of popular games.

9.Consolidating the efforts of NGOs and institutions concerned with popular games.

Photo Appendix

'Al-Wannasah' A wooden doll with hairs made from clay beads. Its body is sculptured in the shape of a row with two small hands. The doll is 23 cms in tallness. It dates back to the 11th dynasty of the middle pharaonic state. (1)

Three Dancing Dwarfs found in the tomb of a girl named Ḥebbi. Each of them is fixed on a round base. Their legs are ornamented with anklets. They are held by strings to a reel that is used to move them. They are realistically sculptured with some deformed bodies and bent legs with highly expressive features on their faces. Several necklaces of the 12th dynasty adorn them, Fayoum Governorate. Dimensions: width 5. 4cm, length 8. 15, height 8. 7 cm. (2)

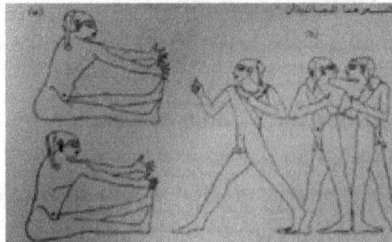

The game 'Shebr We Shebrein' (one and two hndpalm lengths) as represented and portrayed in Kagmni tomb (Old State, saqqarah, Giza Governorate, Egypt)

Nubian children playing with worn out car tyres (West of Aswan Governorate, Egypt, 2004)

A toy in the shape of a doll from Upper Egypt, made by a grandmother to her granddaughter. The head cover and jewelry are well-crafted and bear a lot of details.

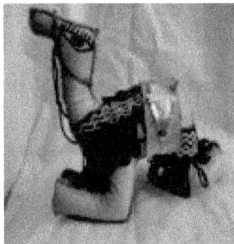

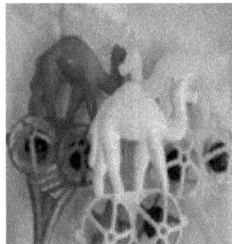

The camel has always been a symbol of patience and beauty for the Arabs. The folkloric craftsman innovated in its formations it whether in craving, embroidery or many various shapes. Various plastic models are created and sold in folkloric Mawaaled (festivals) and at the tombs of devoted religious characters. (AlHussein District, Cairo, April 2012)

The doll *Barby*; the western model for beauty and attractiveness.

The Muslim Fulla which swept over Arab markets. Intelligently, its costume is not particular to a specific local Arab identity; rather it reflects the religious identity. Furthermore, its costume does not give reference to any specific or cultural background. This is, in a sense, an over simplification of Arab Art of doll-making. It is also a stereotyping of Arab methods and patterns of life following western modernity. A noticeable similarity is evident between the two dolls above in both costumes and in their lack of idiosyncrasies.

Chess and backgammon are games of the elderly people who spend their time practicing similar games either in cafes, clubs, and social gatherings or with their friends and peers at home. (1)

The photo is of an Egyptian café which is a popular place where various mental games are practiced. (2)

References

*_____, *Al-MuheeT* .(Dictionary) Magma' al-lughah Al-'Arabeyyah.Vol.2

*_____, *Lisaan Al'Arab* (Lisaan Al'Arab Dictionary)

*_____, *Matn Al-Lughah* (The Explantion of Language)

*'A Group of Researchers', *Tahawwolaat Istratigeyyah (Al-Rabee' Al-Arabi)* (Strategic Changes: The Arab Spring) International Politics Magazine, Al-Ahram Center, Cairo, 2012

*'Abdulfattah MosTafa, *Al-Finoun Al-Tashkileyyah Wa Al-TaTbiqeyyah Litanmeyat Al-Mogtama' Wa al-Insaan Fi Al-'OŠour Al-Qadeemah Wa Al-Woŝtah* (Plastic and Applied Arts in The Development of Society and Man in Ancient and Middle Ages). Dar Al-Ma'aref,1979

*'AbdullaTif Muhammad Khalifah, Sha'abaan Gaballah RaĎwan, *Al-ShakhŠeyyah Al-MeŠreyyah Al-Malameĥ Wa Al-Ab'aag; Dirasah Saykologeyyah* (Features and Dimensions of Egyptian Character ;A Psychological Study). Cairo, Dar Gharieb, 1998.

*Abdulhady El-Gohary, *Mu'gmam 'Elm Al-Egtima'* (A Dictionary of Sociology). Maktabat NahĎat Al-Sharq,Cairo, 1980.

*Abdulhamid Hawwas, *Awraq Fi Al-Thaqafah Al-Sha'abeyyah* (Papers in Folkloric Culture). GEBO, 2006

*Abdulmon'im Muhammad Badr, *Dirasaat Fi Al-tanmeyyah Al-Reefeyyah* (Studies in Rural Development). Dar Al-Ma'aref, 1979

*Ahmad Al-Sabbahi Awad Khalil, *Al-Mahaarat Wa Al-Al'aab Al-Sha'abeyyah* (Skills and Popular Games). Dar Al-Kitaab al-'Arabi for publishing. N.D.

*Ahmad Naguib, *Aghani Al-Tefl Al-Sha'abeyyah Fi 21 Lughah Min Lughaat Al-'Aalam* (Popular Children Songs in 21 World Languages). GEBO, Cairo, 1983.

*Alex Mikchelli, *Al-Huweyyah* (Identity). Dar Al-waseem, Damascus,1993

*Amany El-Bayyoumi Darweesh, "*Istikhdaam Al-Barnameg Fi Al-'Amal Ma'a Al-Gama'aat Wa Tanmeyyat Al-Solouk Al-Qeyaadi lilTefl*" ("Using Programmes in Team Work and Developing Leadership Behavior For Children". Ph.D.Thesis,Faculty of Social Work, Helwan University, 1995.

*Arnest Fisher,The Necessity of art.Trans. As'ad Haleem. GEBO, Cairo, 1998

*Arnold Howards, *Art and Society in History.* Dar Al-Kitaab al-'Arabi for Publishing, Cairo. N.D.

*Baheegah Rasheed, *Aghani Wa Al'aab Sha'abeyyah lilaTfaal* (Popular Songs and Games for Children). 'Aalam Alkutub, 1976.

*El-Sayyed 'Ali Shahdah, *AL-Biyah Wa Aham Moshkilatehah* (The Environment and Its Major Importants). Cairo, 2009

*Eman Mahran, *Kibaar Alsin Wa Al-Mawrooth Al-Sha'abi* (Old People and Folklore). Cairo, 2012

*Eman Mahran, *Tanmeyyat Al_heraf Al-Taqleedeyyah Madkhlan lilħifaaz 'Ala Al-huweyyah* (Developing Traditional Crafts: An Approach To Preserve Identity). SCC, Cairo, 2009.

*Fathi AL-Šifnawi, *Madkhal Ila Dirasat Al-Maathoraat Al-Sha'beyyah Al-Ghinaeyyah (Al-Folkloor Al-Ghinaaie)* (An Introduction to Studying Popular Songs in Heritage (Folkloric Songs) SCC, 2001.

*Fawzi Al-'Anteel, *Al-Folkloor Ma Howa?* (What is Folklore?), Dar Al-Ma'aref, Cairo, N.D.

*Gabr Ibrahim Gabr, *Al-Ostoorah Wa Al-Ramz; Mabadi Naqdeyyah Wa TaTbiqaat:Khams 'Ashr Dirasah liKham 'Ashr Naqid* (Myth and the Symbol; Critical Principles and Applications: Fifteen Studies by Fifteen Authors).Baghdad, 1973.

*Ħassan Ħefni, *Al-Huweyyah* (Identity), Cairo, SCC, 2012, p.17

*Ħassan Ħefni, Nietzsche; *The Resistance Philosopher*. Egyptain Philosophic Society, cairo, 2003, pp. 181,192

*Herbert Reed, *Art Today*. Translator: Mohammad Fathi Hassan & Gerges 'Abdo, Cairo, GEBO, 1981

*John Hartley, *Al-Šina'aat Al-Ibda'aeyyah; Kayfa Tontag Al-Thaqafah Fi 'Aalam Al-Teknologia Wa Al-'Awalamah* (Creative Arts: How Cultutre is Produced in The Age of Technology and Globalization). Vol. 2 Translator: Badr Elsayyed Sulimaan Arifaa'ai.'Aalam Al-Ma'arifah, Kuwait, May 2007.

*Kamaal El-Din Hussein, *Al-'Aab Al-ATfaal Al-Ghinaaeyyah* (Melodic Games of Children) Dar Al-Fikr Al-'Arabi, Cairo, 1991

*Khalaf Bisheer, *Al-Huweyyah Wa Al-'Awlamah* (Identity and Globalization) , Al-Shrouk Newspaper, Algeria, 2006. Quoted by Dr.Mohammad 'Abed Al-Gaabry, a speech in the forum "Al-Touraath Wa Taħadeyyat Al-'Asr" (Heritage and Challenges of the Age)

*Khaleefah Ahmad Mohammad, *Al'aab Al-Šibyah Wa Al-Atfaal Fi Al-Sudaan* (Children and Teenagers Games,in The Sudan) GEBO, 2005.

*Lida Fatħallah Gabrawy, *Al-Oghneyyah Al-Sha'beyyah Wa Dorhah Fi Tarbeyyat Al-Tefl Museeqeyyan* (Folkloric Songs and Their Role in The Musical Upbringing of Children) Ph.D.Thesis, Helwan University, 1979

*Mahmoud Al-Basuiony, *Rosoum Al-ATfaal Qabl Al-Madrasah* (Pre-school Children Paintings). Dar Al-Ma'aref, Cairo, 1991

*Mahmoud Al-Basuiony, *Toroq Ta'allom Al-Finoun* (Methods of Learning Art), Dar Al-Ma'aref, Cairo, 1994

*Mahmoud Elshaal, *Adaah Asaaseyyah Lilkashf 'An Al-Ħaqaeq Al-Kawneyyah Wa Al-Qeyam Al-Gamaleyyah Magallat Al-Finoun Al-Sha'beyyah* (A Basic Tool for Recognizing Universal Facts and Aesthetic Values). Magllat Al-Finoun Al-Sha'beyyah (Folkloric Arts Magazine). Vol. 24, GEBO, Cairo,1989

*Mahmoud Oudah, *Al-Takayyof Wa Al-Muqawamah,Al-Gozoor El-Egtima'eyyah Wa Al-Seyaaseyyah LilshakhŠeyyah Al-MaŠreyyah* (Adaptation and Resistence;The Political and Social Roots of The Egyptian Character) SCC, 1995

*Mohammad 'Adel Khattab, *Al-Al'aab Al-Reefeyyah Al-Sha'beyyah* (Rural Popular Games). The Anglo-Egyptian Bookshop, 1964

*Mohammad 'Emraan, *Al'aab Al-ATfaal Wa Aghaneehah Fi Masr* (Children and Their Songs in Egypt), Silsilat Al-Dirasaat Al-Sha'beyyah(Folkloric Studies Series). GoCP, 2003

*Mohammad Ahmad Abdullah Ibrahim, *Madkhal Fi Al-Al'aab Al-Šagheerah* (An Introductionto Small Games). Al-Mutahidoon LilTeba'ah, Zagazig, 2005

*Mohammad Almunir, *Al'awlamah Wa 'Aalam Bila Huweyyah* (Globalization and A World without Identity). 2000

*Mohammad Anwar Shokri, *Al-Fan Al-MeŠri Al-QaĎeemian* (Ancient Egypt Art) Al-Muasassah Al-MeŠreyyah Al-'Ammah for Writing and Publishing, Cairo, N.D.

*Mohammad Disouki Hamed, *TaTwoor Tareeqat Khedmat Al-Gama'ah Fi Ďowe Barnameg KhaŠkhaŠ Al-Iqtisaad Al-Qawmi* (The Development of Group Work Under The Privitization of National Economy). Tenth Scientific Conference, Faculty of Social Work, Helwan University, 1997.

*Mohammad Hassan Ghanim, *Ghinaa Al-ATfaal* (Children's Songs). Silsilat Al-Dirasaat Al-Sha'beyyah(Folkloric Studies Series). GoCP, 2011.

*Mohsen Atteyah, *Al-Fan Wa 'Aalam Al-Ramz* (Art and The world of Symbols) Dar Al-Ma'aref, Cairo, 1993

*Muhammad Al-Gohari, Dirasaat Fi 'Elm Al-Folkloor *(Studies in Folklore)* Dar Ain for Anthropological Studies and Researches,quoted in Mohammad Al-Gohari et.el. *Qamus El-Ethnologia Wa Al-Folkloor* (Dictionary of Ethnology and Folklore). N.D.

*Philip Spring, *Al-Ramzeyyah Fi Loghat Al-Adyaan Wa Al-Hayah* (Symolism in Life and Liturgical Language). Translated in Damascus, 1992

*Qasim 'Abdouh Qasim, *Al-Muslimoon Wa Ouroppa ;Al-TaTawor Al-Tareekhi LiŠourat Al-Aakhar* (Muslims and Europe; Development of the ther's Image over History). GEBO. 2012. p. 187

*Saad Al-khadem, *Al-Fan Al-Sha'abi Wa Al-Mo'ataqadat Al-Sehreyyah* (Folkloric Art and Magical Beliefs). Maktabat Al-NahĎah, Cairo, N.D.

*Saad Al-Khadem, *Al-Azyaa Al-Sha'abeyyah Wa Al-Finoun Al-Sha'abeyyah Fi al-Nubah* (Folkloric Arts and Costumes in Nubia). GoCP, Cairo, 2005.

*Sameh Maqaar, *AŠl Al-AlffaŽ Al-'Aammah Bayn Al-Lughah Al-Mesreyyah Al-Qadimah* (The Origin of Common Word in Ancient Egyptian Language). GEBO, 2005.

*The Glorious Quran

*Turkki Al-Ḥammad, *Al-Tahqafah Al-'Arabeyyah Fi 'Asr Al-'Awlamah* (Arab Culture in the Age of Globalization). Dar Al-Saqi, Beirut, 2001.

*Viola Albiblawy, *Magallat 'Alam Al-Fikr* (The World of Intellect). Kuwait, vol. 10, 3rd ed., 1979

*Waheeb Mohammad Labeeb, *Al-Al'aab Al-Sha'beyyah Wa Dawrohah Fi Tansheat Al-Tefl Fi Al-Marhalah Al-Senneyyah Min (6-12) Sanah: Dirashah Maydaneyyah Liba'Ď Qura Muhafazat Al-Sharqehyyqueah* (Popular Games and Their Role in Upbringing Children in The Age Group (6-12) years: A Survey Study of Some Villages in Sharqyyah Governorate) Ph.D Thesis The High Institute of Theatre, Art Academy, Cairo, 1998

*WWW.EternalEgypt.Org

*Yuluis Leebes, *AŠl Al-Ashyaa:Bedayaat Al-Thaqafah Al-Insaneyyah* (The Origin of Things:The Beginnings of Human Culture) Translator: Kamel Ismail, Damascus, Dar Al-Mada for Culture and Publishing, 1988

Works by The Author

Iman_a_mahran@hotmail.com

*Younis Al.Qadi; The Lyrical composer of Egyptian Anthem in the Age of
   Enlightenment, General Organization of Cultural Palaces (GOCP), Egypt, 2012
*Elderly People and Folkloric Legacy, Anglo-Egyptian Bookshop, Egypt, 2012
*The Folklore of Jerusalem between Development and Judiazation, Egypt, 2012
*A Minaret in the Shoulder of A Cross ;A documentary study about the art of Kelims
   (Rugs) in Asuit, General Egyptian Book Organization (Gebo), Egypt, 2011
* A Reading in the Memory of the Nation (A Encyclopedia of Lyric Composers in
   Two Centuries),General Egyptian Book Organization (Gebo), Egypt,2 007
*Folkloric Pottery in Qena,General Organization of Cultural Palaces, Egypt, 2007
* Sculptures of Children in The Village of Al.Qarnah, Egypt, 2006
* The Guru of Lyric Composers ; Mohammad Younis Al.Qadhi, Egypt, 2004
*Garagous Potter, The Anglo-Egyptian Bookshop, Egypt, 2003
Under Publication
*Si.Si The Queen of The South and The Imazighen Prince, A Novel from Ancient
   Africa
*Documenting and Developing Folkloric Games, A Case Study from Egyptian
   Environment
*Masterpieces of Folkloric Creation in Upper Egypt, (Vol. I)

www.ingramcontent.com/pod-product-compliance
Lightning Source LLC
Chambersburg PA
CBHW062146020426
42334CB00020B/2537